Spiritual Megatrends

Earl Paulk

Unless otherwise noted, all scripture quotations in this book are from **The New King James Version.**

Copyright 1988
Kingdom Publishers
Atlanta, Georgia

Printed in the United States of America
ISBN 0-917595-16-5

DEDICATION

To the
Students and Faculty
of
Harvester Academy
and
Earl Paulk School of Biblical Studies

May the hours of planting God's truth in your minds and hearts reap bountifully as you experience the joy of harvest through the lives of those who come to know Him by your witness.

FOREWORD
by Tricia Weeks

I am one of the *Baby Boomers*. I cut my teeth on lessons in life from a daily diet of *Mickey Mouse Club*. I am typical of my generation. Generally, most of us grew up with positive expectations, optimism toward the future and clear cut social and religious values.

We trusted the answers we were given and believed the American dream. We respected our teachers. We earned our Sunday School attendance buttons and our Girl and Boy Scout badges. We saluted the flag, studied hard and spoke with pride about family, school and country. At great sacrifice to themselves, my parents insisted that I get a college diploma as an insurance policy against all obstacles and despair in life. I prepared well. Life was good, and the future was bright.

What happened? The Beatles sang, "There's gonna' be a revolution . . ." and they were right. Combine violent riots, a controversial war, scandals surrounding our leaders, assassinations, drugs, free love and social demonstrations with the mindset of youth who have been pampered, instantly gratified and promised the moon.

What do you get? Disillusionment. Throwaway relationships. Shattered hopes. New questions for which the old answers just don't seem to work. Now the theme songs of many in my generation have lyrics like, "I did it my way," a sad consolation for broken promises and broken hearts in a crazy, mixed-up world.

When I joined Chapel Hill Harvester Church in 1980, I had spent the 70's hoping for the Rapture. I was a "Charismatic" Presbyterian who taught high school English. I had distributed boxes of Hal Lindsey's books to my students. I knew the truth of the Bible. The world was in trouble, and I intended to take everyone I could with me at that trumpet sound. I was drawn to Chapel Hill when many of the *hard cases* among my students were transformed into Bible-carrying crusaders for the Lord. Miracles have a way of getting your attention.

At Chapel Hill I learned about a new revolution. So many of the expectations and goals made me remember those happy television families like *the Cleavers* and the *the Nelsons,* but with some exciting differences. My perfectly charted timetable for the end of the world was suddenly challenged by a strong emphasis on understanding the totality of God's Word.

Yes, Jesus is surely coming. As much as ever I want to spend eternity with as many people as possible. But along with assurance of the precious gift of eternal life in the heavenly realm, the realization slowly began to sink in that I might have a few unfinished details to take care of right here—both for my sake and the sake of the world Jesus loves.

Old concepts die hard. Many times I've wrestled, searched the Bible and prayed over specific points in

Bishop Earl Paulk's sermons. God has always answered the questions of my heart. Nothing surpasses the joy of having pieces of a complicated puzzle begin to fit together in simplicity and clarity.

Earl Paulk's preaching and the Holy Spirit's teaching has helped me to understand biblical reality. Beyond Church traditions, misinterpretations, idealism and theories is a real Kingdom of God filled with unshakeable righteousness, peace and joy—a Kingdom *at hand* now, and a government manifested fully at the coming of Christ.

Meanwhile, there's work to do. I joined the staff of Chapel Hill in 1983 as Bishop Earl Paulk's editorial assistant. Bishop Paulk is a man who lives what he preaches. His books rattle sleeping churches the way his sermons rattle sleeping Christians. Some say he walks the *cutting edge*. I will vouch for the spiritual challenge he ignites in anyone who gets near him. Certain people are gifted by God in calling forth the gifts in others, stirring them up, getting them moving. Earl Paulk is such a man.

Spiritual Megatrends speaks to Christians of any generation, but it has particular significance to those of us who have grown up in the historical whirlwind of the last forty years. I believe that the cry of my generation is for spiritual reality. We are no longer buying slick hype, empty promises or tickets to religious shows. Too many ivory towers have crumbled. We're tired of platitudes from Bible-waving phonies who play church. We only buy dreams worth dying for, because only those dreams are worth the price of investing our lives. This time we tread on hard, cold reality, enlisted as spiritually empowered soldiers fighting for a good life and a bright future. His truth is marching on . . .

Chapter One
Spiritual Trends

† The trumpet of the Holy Spirit sounds around the world today with an urgency to "make all things ready."

† God is positioning His Church for the great harvest. Networking of ministry around the world is sovereignly strategic to accomplish God's master plan.

† The scope of world problems on our shrinking planet demands that Christians adopt a world view of ministry.

† The Church is comprehending her identity as an army engaged in warfare.

† As secular society realizes that the problems of mankind will not be solved by science, politics, education or money, God will give the Church wisdom and solutions to the perplexities of our age, igniting an unsurpassed witness of the gospel of the Kingdom to the world.

† Denominational walls will continue to fall—making the prayer of Jesus for oneness (John 17) a reality.

† The Church, both liberals and conservatives from all orthodox theological persuasions, will increasingly re-alize the need to re-evaluate their traditions with a fresh examination of 1. scriptural interpretation, 2. church structure and 3. worship forms.

† In every aspect of secular accomplishment—music, science, business, politics, beauty, sports, education, etc.—the Church will become a visible standard of righteousness by which world systems will be judged.

† Kingdom against kingdom confrontations will steadily increase and the lines will be more clearly drawn between forces of *darkness* and forces of *light*.

† As world systems crumble, the Church will be positioned by God to offer society the only source of hope, restoration and direction.

† As Christians realize that the demonstration of the gospel of the Kingdom as a witness is our assignment before the coming of Christ, the Church will mobilize quickly to fulfill this great commission.

1

A NEW REFORMATION

I am a descendant of a long line of preachers and farmers. When I was a child, my dad, a classical Pentecostal preacher in the Church of God, insisted that I work on my granddaddy's farm in south Georgia in the summertime. Daddy had worked on the farm before God called him into the ministry. He realized that hard work in the fields would teach me valuable lessons about life as well as channel my boundless energy in a positive direction.

I remember the rain on a tin roof during those summer visits to Granddaddy Tomberlin's farm. I always slept on the side porch of the little farmhouse. Early in the morning, Granddaddy Tomberlin would organize his workers for the day. I'll never forget waking up to a tone of urgency in Granddaddy's voice.

"Go to the neighboring farms and tell them I need all the workers they can spare today! I've got to get the crop in today! I need workers!"

If the fodder wasn't gathered in time, it would rot on the stalk. Many days we worked against time to salvage all the overripe crops that we could. Nature teaches important lessons of timing—planting, fertilizing, cultivating, weeding, and then finally, urgent reaping of a ripe harvest.

The universal Church in our world today—a spiritually defined collection of individuals who have been born by the Spirit of God through faith in Jesus Christ's atoning death and resurrection—hears a voice of urgency calling for laborers to reap the great harvest of the earth before the coming of the Lord. While skeptics say, "All things remain as they were . . ." the spiritual wind is blowing. Spiritual ears are hearing a trumpet blast a certain sound of alarm, proclaiming the fullness of God's intentions for this historical hour. What is God saying? "I need laborers in the harvest! Send Me all the workers you can find to harvest the fields that are ripe."

In 1960, a key passage of Scripture became the cornerstone of the ministry at Chapel Hill Harvester Church in Atlanta.

> But when He saw the multitudes, He was moved with compassion for them, because they were weary and scattered, like sheep having no shepherd. Then He said to His disciples, "The harvest truly is plentiful, but the laborers are few. Therefore pray the Lord of the harvest to send out laborers into His harvest." (Matthew 9:36-38)

The Lord of the harvest is now positioning His laborers around the globe. God's strategy for harvest is quickly surfacing into reality. I don't apologize for stating firmly that Chapel Hill Harvester Church in Atlanta is one of many places where God is raising up laborers to share in His plan for human history. That realization only means that we must walk carefully in our accountability and responsibility before God. We labor as those called by God to love and to restore *scattered sheep* with the transforming power of Christ.

Though our ministry was prophetically named *Harvesters,* hundreds, thousands, an innumerable throng of Baptists, Presbyterians, Methodists, Catholics, Pentecostals—all churches where Jesus is Lord—are training disciples to proclaim and demonstrate the gospel of Jesus Christ around the world as dedicated laborers in this hour of spiritual enlistment. Many ears hear the wind of the Spirit! Many hearts know the urgency of this hour!

Amid the clamor of confusing religious noises— clanging brass and tinkling cymbals—the voice of the bride is also heard speaking with confidence and authority. The bride boldly speaks the Word of God into the atmosphere to visible (people) and invisible (spirits) beings. Just as creation responded to God's voice in its formation (Genesis 1), all of creation now groans, awaiting the manifestation of a Church speaking in the name and the authority of the Creator. Out of chaos and confusion, God utters His voice and establishes order and design.

A voice of authority speaks to the dead and calls forth life. Jesus called forth Lazarus from the tomb (John 11:43). Ezekiel spoke over dead, dry bones which became a great army (Ezekiel 37:10). Many

Christians and their churches are waking up from a long sleep resembling spiritual death. These Christians hear the call to march in step with a powerful army ready to battle every stronghold opposing God's eternal plan. They are breaking the curse of silence by proclaiming the gospel of the Kingdom.

> . . . the voice of joy and the voice of gladness, the voice of the bridegroom and the voice of the bride, the voice of those who will say: "Praise the Lord of hosts, For the Lord is good, For His mercy endures forever"—and of those who will bring the sacrifice into the house of the Lord. For "I will cause the captives of the land to return as at the first," says the Lord . . . (Jeremiah 33:11)

THE FUTURISTS

I have read with interest many contemporary books (both secular and ecclesiastical) analyzing current events and making predictions about the future of life on our planet. The economic, political and social forecasters have tremendous insights into trends influencing our world in the next few decades. Indeed, we live in very interesting times!

Technological advances have drowned us in a deluge of information. Mass communication opens our minds to signals in the air at the push of a button. As never before, people on different hemispheres are intricately connected to one another—economically, politically, spiritually. Still, the technology for communication does little to ensure true understanding among people residing on earth.

The nations of our shrinking globe clash in continuous strife. Domestic conflicts of small nations impose their influence upon the policies of the super powers. Paradoxically, sophisticated communications fail even in solving the isolation of the soul of an individual. Although surrounded by so many forms of communication, people still live in isolation with broken hearts. No historical period has provided more evidence than this one that the majority of people in our world live out their lives as captives of inner loneliness and fear.

An objective overview of life on our planet forces one to admit that scientists, politicians and educators do not seem to be able to solve the mammoth complications of our existence. We expected solutions to famine and cures for diseases by now. We believed that we had learned enough lessons from previous wars to pursue peace—yet war continues. We should have learned lessons on avoiding a failing economy from our past mistakes, yet the world economy totters. The ominous threat of terrorism increases. Natural disasters—earthquakes, drought, volcanic eruptions—override the advantages of sophisticated detection devices as they continue to wipe out entire cities, destroying in moments thousands of lives and the steel monuments men have erected with pride.

In considering contemporary futurists' predictions, I have sorted through them, agreed with some and disagreed with others. I do not claim to be a scientist, an economist or a sociologist. Yet over forty years of ministry and counseling experience qualifies me professionally to verify or to dispute the findings of social scientists and educators who make predictions about the future. I leave the statistical data gathering to them. As a student of mankind, I frequently use their research to draw certain conclusions and to confirm my own theories. My conclusions are always based primarily upon the principles and precepts of God's Word.

SPIRITUAL TRENDS

A caring ministry needs to utilize the most current information that professional researchers can provide to remain effective in ministering to the needs of people. Times change. Human nature does not change. Indeed, the principles of creation woven throughout God's Word transcend time. However, theologians of the past never wrestled with the moral implications of organ transplants, artificial organs, artificial insemination, space exploration, cosmetic surgery, etc.

Principles governing human responses to life's circumstances are unchanging. For example, despite our sophisticated technology, the pregnancy of Hagar by Abraham opens discussion on the moral implications surrounding the plight of surrogate mothers! Emotional responses are timeless. Mary, despite the visitation from an angel, faced the same social pressures that an unmarried teenage girl who is pregnant faces in the twentieth century. The issues surrounding sibling rivalry began with the sons of Adam and Eve.

Most pastors are sensitive to spiritual trends in ministry. A variety of influences have provided me with the opportunity to study the trends of various theological persuasions. As I have said, I grew up in the home of a Pentecostal pastor. I graduated from a Baptist college (Furman University) and a Methodist seminary (Candler School of Theology, Emory University).

Chapel Hill Harvester Church in Atlanta is an interdenominational church. Members of CHHC have come from various theological perspectives ranging from classical Pentecostals to Roman Catholics and everything else in between. Our current church parish of more than ten thousand people is racially, politically, socially and educationally diverse—a combination which produces a beautiful symphony of praise and worship to God.

Chapel Hill Harvester Church demonstrates variety with loving unity through redemption in Jesus Christ. Our theology is orthodox according to the historical creeds and foundational tenets of Scripture. This blend of cultural and denominational perspectives in one congregation is unique. For this reason, numerous ministries have called us a *cutting edge* church, a *lead domino* ministry, a *forerunner.*

Regularly our International Department receives firsthand reports concerning the Marxist tactics of liberation theology from ministries that battle that ideology in Nicaragua, Chile, El Salvador, Costa Rica and other Latin American nations. A musical drama, *The Bride,* written from the teaching of the Kingdom message preached from my pulpit, recently sold out a city auditorium for five nights in Cape Town, South Africa. This past year our ministry sent one of our associate pastors and his wife to South Africa, and two other associate pastors to Central America on fact-finding missions. We recently hosted an international pastors' conference attended by several hundred Church leaders from twenty-five nations.

My covering in ministry is the College of Bishops in the International Communion of Charismatic Churches which includes Bishop Robert McAlister from Brazil, Bishop Benson Idahosa from Nigeria, Bishop Herro Blair from Jamaica, Bishop John Meares from Washington, D.C., and Bishop Harry Mushegan, also from Atlanta. Together we are privileged to provide spiritual eldership to hundreds of churches worldwide.

Am I presumptuous in assuming that God has allowed me to detect future trends of the Church? Such an assumption is certain to seem presumptuous to some of the critics analyzing the teaching of current Christian teachers. Yet we know from Scripture that men of God were both astonished and humbled whenever God trusted them to glimpse the future.

Some trends I will discuss are quite obvious to anyone who reads the Scriptures and keeps abreast of current discussions in theological circles. Jesus spoke plainly about many aspects of history that we see happening in the Church today. We know the season of the coming of the Lord. Still, Jesus indicated that He had many more things to tell His disciples which the Spirit would teach them when He came. Jesus promised that the Holy Spirit would guide them into all truth and tell them things to come (John 16:13).

The only acceptable motivation for seeking truth is a desire to be in covenant with God. Knowing and doing God's will is essential to manifesting the Kingdom of God on earth as it is in heaven. The power of Christ living within us is a great mystery or sacrament. The Spirit of the Lord brings healing, restoration and overcoming power to our mortal flesh. The reality of restoration and overcoming power is the "good news" which Jesus preached (Luke 4:18,19).

A NEW DAY

Jesus said, "He who has an ear to hear, let him hear what the Spirit says to the churches." The Church has come to a new crossroad. Like it or not, ready or not, the Pentecostal outpouring of the Holy Spirit at the turn of the century began opening God's people to truth from God's Word which disregards walls built by denominations, doctrinal differences or religious traditions. Today those of us who are the fruit of that outpouring see new, glorious horizons in view. Human nature inevitably resists changes which challenge comfortable traditions. The greatest enemy to a future move of God is the strict adherence to a present move of God.

From Genesis into the twentieth century God's people always encounter opposition to any new direction that God speaks to ears that are sensitive to His voice. The Old Testament history of Israel provides types, shadows and patterns for Christians. Church history proves that whenever someone hears from God and initiates changes in worship forms, teaching emphases from Scripture or structure in ministry, their first test of validity is enduring intense persecution from people insisting on maintaining established patterns.

Let me state emphatically that the new move in the Church today is new only in its emphasis and implementation. I believe that many modern Christians have embraced the challenge to demonstrate the mandates of Scripture. It's amazing how the expectations of Christianity have strayed from God's simple instructions.

Jesus said that His Kingdom comes through violent men who take it by force (Matthew 11:12). Persecution purifies the motives of people who embrace a move of God. Jesus also instructed us to live as spiritual *peacemakers,* "wise as serpents and harmless as doves" (Matthew 10:16). That paradox in motivation produces radical love in Christian witnesses. The greatest strategy for the Church to use to accomplish her mission from God is the strategy of love (1 Corinthians 13). When people listen to God and move by the power of the Holy Spirit, all opposition to God's plan, no matter how powerful or pronounced, is ultimately in vain.

Today God is speaking clear direction to Christians who seek Him and live with the establishment of His Kingdom on earth as their first priority in the choices they make. Such a witness causes walls blocking the move of the Holy Spirit, like the walls of Jericho, to topple. Some people easily hear with anointed ears and willingly obey the voice of the Lord. Others resist change and discipline by kicking stubbornly against the goad.

Three areas of intense discussion in this time of enlistment in the harvest will be 1. scriptural interpretation, 2. church structure and 3. worship forms. Unfolding mysteries, fresh illumination into God's anointed Word, indicate that we live in an age of tremendous opportunity and responsibility to communicate and demonstrate the gospel of the Kingdom to the world. Many Christians realize that neither an *escapist* mentality nor an *otherworld* focus will ever produce that empowered holy nation of kings and priests which God has called His Church to be in the world.

How do we fill the earth with the knowledge of the Lord while we sing about "cabins in the corner of Gloryland"? What kind of witness is *an escape* from problems when we are called *overcomers* according to God's Word? We are to live as demonstrations of responsible Christianity. How do we move as a spiritual army unless we understand the full work of the fivefold ministry in edifying believers? Many Christians accept the ministry of evangelists, pastors and teachers, but where are the God-called apostles and prophets in the Church today? How can an army be effective if it is unable to identify its leaders?

A generation demonstrating an adequate witness of the gospel of the Kingdom will experience the return of Jesus Christ (Matthew 24:14). This long awaited culmination of history depends on the obedience of spiritually enlightened generations who will fully follow the Lord as Caleb did in entering the promised land.

The world can never be judged until people recognize a choice between God's will and worldly standards of living. God's yardstick for measurement is Jesus Christ's perfect example for us, an exemplary life of one man who became the example of the life of His mature Church in the world. How can God judge jealousy in the world when the Church continues to be competitive? How can God judge greed in the world when the Church continues to serve mammon?

Christians must live out lifestyles which demonstrate Jesus' Kingdom principles as workable solutions—not by might nor by (human) power, but by (the power of) the Holy Spirit. Kingdom principles drastically contrast worldly concepts in politics, finance, the arts, education, sports, etc. A spiritual demonstration in these areas—exposing worldly concepts by contrasting them with God's ways, the fruit of His Spirit—offers people choices. They receive a witness of the Kingdom of God so that they are forced to choose. A clear choice between God's Kingdom and earthly kingdoms sets the standards by which God will judge the world for whatever choices people make.

The Kingdom of God on earth is an alternative to totally replace world systems at the return of Jesus Christ. I do not believe that man will, nor could fully manifest the Kingdom of God on earth through human efforts before Christ returns. I disclaim any association with the old "manifest sons of God" movement or the humanistic dogma of the New Age which are based upon beliefs which I have no reason to defend. A counterfeit only indicates that the real exists somewhere.

Man's works are incapable of impacting the world with the dynamic witness that laborers in God's harvest will know through the power of the Holy Spirit. The total redemption of mortal flesh occurs at the coming of Christ, when the mortal takes on immortality in the twinkling of an eye (1 Corinthians 15:50-53). Until then, works of the flesh will only manifest the presence of Christ's Kingdom, but spiritual fruit remains throughout eternity (John 15:16).

We've often reacted to the failures of movements and error in doctrines by backing away from the unchangeable truth of God's Word. The Bible says that "creation groans" for the manifestation of the Holy Spirit in the lives of believers (Romans 8). A Kingdom witness in the harvest depends upon the power of the Holy Spirit within Christians, the outward manifestation of "Christ in us, the hope of glory!" Fruit of such manifestations is easily discerned because it stands the test of time. Seeking the Kingdom always produces righteousness, peace and joy in the Holy Spirit. Spiritual fruit gives glory to God and unveils the identity of Jesus Christ to the world.

The Church must live as the body of Christ in the world. That statement is so simple and yet so profound. Until the Church manifests a true demonstration of Christ's character, intentions and power to restore "that which was lost" as Jesus did, the Church merely spins her wheels, gazes into the heavens, forms committees and keeps her programs going. For too long the Church has waited passively for a Bridegroom Who is held as a King in exile until the restoration of all things (Acts 3:21).

MISSING PIECES OF A PUZZLE

Why was the Holy Spirit given to the Church at Pentecost? I am convinced that God had much more in mind in empowering His disciples than producing good citizens who quietly go about their business, attend church regularly, hold respectable jobs, raise polite children, pay their taxes and put twenty dollars in the offering plate each week. Such Christians are certainly commendable citizens among the majority of people in secular society. Their lives represent a witness for God in contrast to people who live without discipline or direction. But the question must be answered as to whether they are fulfilling the mission of the empowered Church in the world. How do their lives compare to the life of Christ Who is their standard, their example? Do they show the same unconditional love for redeeming the world that Christ demonstrated by His obedience to God even through His death on the cross? Do they weep over cities that refuse to hear the voice of God's will for them?

The body of Christ becomes that standard of righteousness, as the story of Job depicts, to powers and principalities (Job 1; Ephesians 3:10). Furthermore, anyone who believes that "Jesus did it all for us and we must hold on until He comes to rescue us out of this mess" must answer the scriptural reasons that Jesus gave the fivefold ministry to equip the Church. Equip us for what purpose? To hold on (as survivors) until He comes, or to live as overcomers?

> And He Himself gave some to be apostles, some prophets, some evangelists, and some pastors and teachers, for the equipping of the saints for the work of ministry, for the edifying of the body of Christ, till we all come to the unity of the faith and the knowledge of the Son of God, to a perfect man, to the measure of the stature of the fullness of Christ. (Ephesians 4:11-13)

Admittedly, the full realization of this goal—unity of faith, knowledge of the Son of God, a perfect man, the measure of the stature of the fullness of Christ—is yet to be realized in the Church. Some Christian teachers believe it is heresy to say that it should be realized! If it is to be realized only when Christ comes, why is it promised in the context of the work of the fivefold ministry? Would God's Word promise this reality if it were unattainable in this world? I contend that every Christian will answer that question with personal accountability in the next few decades!

Christians who understand the Church's identity and goals in the world challenge "the gates of hell." They are a threat to satanic forces and are registered in the heavens to do warfare (Acts 19:15). As highly disciplined soldiers fighting with spiritual weapons of faith, *violent men* of the Kingdom will not back away from fulfilling their callings from God. Accusers will seek to discredit them through intimidation, innuendos, accusations and unorthodox associations. Kingdom against kingdom confrontations are inevitable *trends* of the last days according to Jesus (Matthew 24:7). Prepare for and expect them. But remember that God's army never wins battles using conventional weapons. Our weapons are not carnal. We will examine the subject of spiritual warfare in greater detail throughout this book.

Even in the most recent blights upon a Christian witness to the world with media coverage focused upon numerous scandals in the Christian community, we must discern God's purposes for His Church amid the confusion and shameful details. Many times the obvious judgments are not the way God views a situation at all. Pharisaical judgments are as sinful to God as bribery and adultery. Sin is sin. Reactions to someone's sin can be as damaging as the obvious sinful act—as with those who were ready to stone the woman taken in adultery (John 8:3-5). When a Christian's sins are exposed, the reaction to that disclosure becomes such a test of spiritual maturity for every Christian. We must feel and speak with the mind of Christ. But know this: everything that can be shaken must be and will be shaken!

Babylon will grow worse and worse and will finally fall. Few people would argue with the statement that pestilence upon society such as AIDS, blatant immorality and psychic phenomena from occult practices are all too commonplace. Our world is gripped with fear! In the Church's greatest hour of enlistment, we are experiencing those prophetic words, ". . . men's hearts failing them from fear and the expectation of those things which are coming on the earth . . ." (Luke 21:26).

THE GOSPEL OF HOPE

Arise, shine; For your light has come! And the glory of the Lord is risen upon you. For behold, the darkness shall cover the earth, and deep darkness the people; But the Lord will arise over you, and His glory will be seen upon you. (Isaiah 60:1,2)

25

In the new reformation by the Holy Spirit, Christians will no longer be "tossed to and fro" by traditions or doctrines which prevent the unity of our witness in this critical hour in history. The voice of the Holy Spirit is our guide and brings us into unity of mind and heart. The bride of Christ waits aggressively for the coming of the Bridegroom. She is a light, a city set upon a hill, contrasting the darkness covering the people of the world. The description, "set upon a hill," implies great visibility.

I do not mean to imply that the new reformation by the Spirit will necessarily cause all Christians to agree in every area of biblical interpretation. *Covenant with God* becomes the central issue. Among God's covenant people are a diversity and variety of worship forms. Covenant people vary on certain issues of biblical interpretation. They may even adhere to a variety of church traditions without violating spiritual unity as long as they maintain basic principles of covenant with God: repentance, water baptism, the Lord's table, tithing, church attendance, and recognizing spiritual headship.

The one uncompromising issue of covenant with God focuses on Jesus Christ as the chief Cornerstone, the revelation of God in the flesh. The revelation of Jesus is the unequivocal rock of the Church. Christians must stand together on the rock of His revelation to face the world as His witnesses in demonstration, power and oneness, "that the world may know" that Christ has come (John 17:23). That binding ingredient is love, the proof that Jesus said would identify His true disciples (John 13:35).

Throughout Scripture, God requires two witnesses to establish truth. Jesus was that first witness revealing the Father, coming to earth as Emmanuel, God is with us. Now like never before in history, the Church, Christ's body on the earth, must shine as that second witness, revealing the Son so that He may come to judge the world and rule as King of kings and Lord of lords. This *witness principle* far transcends a limited concept of evangelism as only leading people to salvation in Christ. The lifestyle of Christians, a living demonstration of Kingdom principles in daily life, is the true witness of the gospel of the Kingdom.

Perhaps the enemies of God are forcing men of good will together. For example, could it be that the disintegration of the family in modern society will serve as a common denominator for people who love family life to join forces. Think of those whose roots are in *family togetherness*—Jews, Catholics, Charismatics and even conservative political coalitions for the protection of the family—coming together to war against drugs, pornography, abortion, unjust tax laws, etc.

Jesus said that in the last days He would send prophets, wise men and scribes to proclaim the coming of His Kingdom (Matthew 23:34). Prophets direct God's people with His Word. They unfold scriptural mysteries and impart God's strategy in warfare to lead God's people victoriously through end time events. God does nothing without speaking His direction through His prophets (Amos 3:6,7).

Wise men are solution-oriented believers, as Joseph and Daniel became to their generations. These anointed men were called before rulers to give answers from God to save their nations. They issued warnings and interpreted signs. They offered workable solutions to the problems their rulers faced. Modern wise men of the Kingdom—many of them professional men and women—will offer solutions and alternatives to the methods of world systems. They will speak simple solutions given to them by the Holy Spirit to solve some of the most complex problems confounding our world today. They will boldly honor the Lord in their solutions and reveal the source of their wisdom as being the Lord.

Scribes are communicators who interpret and record the signs of their times. Many will come into the work of the Kingdom from the secular media. Spiritually anointed scribes understand and discern truth amid the chaos of seemingly senseless events in history. Scribes are able to bring a consensus to the prophetic past, evaluate contemporary events and project future trends and direction according to God's Word. They are anointed with prophetic understanding.

The new reformation of the Spirit addresses seven areas which the Church must comprehend by spiritual enlightenment. Natural understanding will never comprehend the new reformation by the Spirit; it can only evaluate its results. Remember, the Holy Spirit guides us into all truth. Those who read God's Word with natural understanding will oppose the move of God in these areas because they will never understand its purpose. But the implementation of these directives throughout the universal Church by Christians with transformed minds will quickly ignite a world changing witness. We stand on the brink of that day!

Allow me to emphasize again that spiritual unity among believers can never be accomplished through organizations, conclaves or man-made structure. Ministries emphasizing unity are often attacked because the idea of Christian unity has been so maligned by humanistic groups such as the New Age.

Nevertheless, unity is necessary for the witness of God's people before the coming of the Lord. Widespread misunderstanding of unity now hinders the fulfillment of God's plan among born-again believers.

INGREDIENTS OF ENLIGHTENMENT

1. *God's people must clearly understand God's purposes for planet earth, outlined in the book of Genesis.* Unless spiritual direction moves in accordance with God's original intentions at creation, we simply waste time and effort. God's plan has not changed. The Church is God's garden in the world to bring correction to worldly chaos, taking dominion in God's authority. From the beginning, God has desired to give His authority to a man or a nation who lives in proper relationship to Him.

2. *God's people must understand the difference between positional and spiritual authority.* Spiritual authority is influence with God. Positional authority is necessary for proper structure and implementation of God's will for His people. The universal Church must be viewed as one body in the earth. We must rely on one another's strengths and cover one another's weaknesses. Present-day denominations must be regarded as to the particular theological emphasis they offer other members of Christ's body in the earth. We edify one another to be the adequate witness to the world as *God's covenant people.*

3. *Christians must take a careful look at biblical social order concerning the way God intended for man to relate to his society.* Racial, economic and cultural issues must be addressed by God's people if we are to demonstrate a Kingdom mentality which transcends a particular generation and nationality (time and place). God's Word promises a theocracy

characterized by righteousness and justice (Psalm 89:14). The government which Jesus Christ will eventually establish on earth is a startling contrast to current political ideologies. We must never confuse patriotism or national pride with our commitment to Christ and seeking His Kingdom. God's blessings and anointing are not bound by national boundaries.

4. *The Church of the harvest will implement principles of responsible Christianity.* Attitudes toward lifestyle, finances, education and personal relationships need examining and refining. Christian involvement in public education, government and civic affairs is essential. Our voices will be bold and confident when we are speaking by the power of the Holy Spirit. We must confront humanistic philosophies and expose their fallacies. Responsible Christianity calls for us to address ecological concerns. Our view of the earth becomes very important if we believe that it belongs to God and was created for His glory.

5. *The covenant Church must open spiritual understanding to comprehend God's desires in praise and worship.* Because the love of God is the motivation of worship, His perfect love will cast out fear of various worship forms. The Psalms compel God's people to enter into His presence with singing, clapping, shouting, playing on loud instruments and dancing before the Lord, releasing all energy within them to bless His name.

On the other hand, God is a being with emotions. The mood of the Lord may lead His people into reverent silence, weeping in intercession or bowing before Him to acknowledge His majesty. Spiritual sensitivity to God's emotions is essential in pleasing the Lord. God's people must learn to move as He moves, feeling and responding to the Spirit as He directs them at any given time and place in which they assemble together.

6. *The Church must address the distinction between the Old and New Covenant in Scripture.* Widespread misunderstandings and contradictions in teaching from leaders throughout the Church have resulted not only in confusion, but also in diversion from the major issues facing the Church. The most effective strategies Satan has used against the Church are diversion and delay which ultimately results in deception. Covenant understanding is the foundation of our faith.

Scriptures distinguishing God's covenant with natural Israel from spiritual Israel must be clarified if God's people are to grow to maturity. These issues hinder a proper identity of the Church's role in the world today. I agree that indeed *the fig tree is blooming*. The bride of Christ must fulfill her commission through the New Covenant in Jesus Christ. Jesus is the total fulfillment of the Law and the Prophets. His bride is a living, spiritual nation of kings and priests from every tribe, tongue and nation—including modern Israel.

And God has definitely preserved the natural branch. I believe that the mature Church will provoke the natural Jew toward Israel's Messiah, Jesus Christ. Perhaps the provocation will be as Pastor John Haggee of San Antonio, Texas, puts it, "unconditional love." I anticipate a tremendous ingathering of Jews to profess the New Covenant in the next few years. The Sanhedrin, rabbinical lawyers who have stood at the door of the Kingdom since the time of Christ, will be brought to the knowledge of the Lord through national calamities visited upon Israel before the coming of the Lord.

7. *The Holy Spirit must enlighten believers as to the true meaning of the Kingdom of God in relationship to the Church.* All creation eagerly awaits the *Kingdom within us* to be manifested in the world through our lives. Kingdom truth is a witness only when it is lived out in authority and power in our daily circumstances and spheres of influence.

A new reformation by the Spirit calls for total commitment from individual believers. Of course, truth ultimately wins every test. Individually we must choose to walk the path of truth in a hostile environment. Jesus promised that His followers would receive persecution from the world, but hostility also arises from half-brothers and half-sisters, Christians who resent the desire they recognize in brothers and sisters who continually seek, knock, ask, hunger and thirst to know the Lord more intimately.

The biggest little word in fulfilling God's plan in the Church today is the word *if*. "If My people who are called by My name . . ." "If I be lifted up, I'll draw all men to Myself . . ." "If any two agree as touching anything, it shall be done for them . . ." God's fulfillment of His promises is contingent upon His people's obedience. Remember, we are joint heirs with Christ, Abraham's seed. God requires our complete obedience to His voice through faith in Him. His greatest desire is to hear the voice of His bride in absolute agreement with His will.

The contingent of God's plan rests in our daily choices. Many Christians settle for pottage which satisfies their hunger for the moment, instead of living as people who have an everlasting birthright, heritage and inheritance. At times we are tempted to make choices which gratify and exalt ourselves or one another instead of Jesus. An objective assessment of the Church shows that we're not yet ready to be a bride, much less to rule and reign with Christ. The bride of Christ must learn to pursue her Bridegroom's interest before her own. Keen discernment is essential to grow to maturity.

Immediately after explaining to His disciples the events of the end times, Jesus told two parables (Matthew 25). One parable is the story of five wise and five foolish virgins, emphasizing the necessity of anointing oil in preparing adequately for the coming of the Lord. The second parable warns believers to make use of their talents to glorify the Master. The requirements are greater for those richly gifted by God. Accountability to God requires that we give back to Him. Both of these parables show the need for action from the bride of Christ. Giving to God means meeting the needs of His body. After these two parables, Jesus gives the criterion by which He will judge the nations—how well they responded to the needs of His brethren, the Church.

I rejoice in the quickening power of the new reformation by the Spirit. My ears are open with anticipation. I press with all my heart to enter into the fullness of this hour of destiny. The Kingdom of God is my meat, day and night.

With great love, I reach out to my Pentecostal family who knows the joy of the Lord in worship. I reach out to my Fundamentalist family who adheres to God's Word as their final authority. I extend my hand in fellowship to my brothers and sisters in the ecclesiastical church who bring pageantry and historical wealth to worship in the body of Christ. They give me an awareness of His presence among continuous generations in the history of His Church.

I embrace all brothers and sisters in Jesus Christ: anyone who names the name of Jesus as the Son of God, worships Him in Spirit and Truth, seeks first His Kingdom, and stands solidly, unshakeably upon the Rock of His revelation. None of us alone has all the pieces of the puzzle.

IDENTIFYING THE BRIDE

How do we identify the true bride? How do we know her voice when we hear it?

1. She is in covenant with God. She has entered the secret places of God in intercession and knows His protection by calling upon the covenant between them (Psalm 91).

2. She is doing the work of the Kingdom—loosing the bonds of wickedness, undoing heavy burdens, letting the oppressed go free, breaking every yoke (Isaiah 58). She proclaims the gospel to the poor, *good news* of the acceptable year of the the Lord!

3. Her voice is motivated by love—her tone is not like sounding brass and a tinkling cymbal.

The bride is a stark contrast to those whom the natural mind would reason to be the ones who speak as representatives for God. Vashti was a queen of the flesh. She looked like a queen. On the other hand, Esther was a Jewish girl, an exile, raised by her uncle, Mordecai. Vashti represents the flesh and Esther represents the Spirit bride who prepares herself for the King.

Saul looked like a king, tall and handsome. He was the epitome of what people believed that a king should be—but he disobeyed God's orders. On the other hand, David was the youngest son, a shepherd tending sheep who was almost forgotten by his own father. Clearly, people would have elected Saul to be their ruler over David. Yet God chose David, a man after God's own heart, to demonstrate the Kingdom of praise and establish a Kingdom without end.

Likewise, many will choose to hear the Vashti/Saul churches. They hold Sunday services in every city. Many of them are wealthy and look and sound like they know God. They have position and influence. They have everything they need—except the Spirit of the Lord!

The new reformation of the Spirit is raising up Esther and David churches around the world. They may not look like royalty yet, but they are! What do they have that makes the difference? Anointing. The power of the Holy Spirit. True worship. Love. Covenant understanding that results in discipline, authority and purpose.

I feel the rumblings. God's people are waking to a new day, a new sound, a new vision imparted through a fresh anointing of the Holy Spirit. The bride is waking up, growing up, realizing her identity and sounding the trumpet to announce the "Day of the Lord!" Her voice calls out. Like it or not, prepare to move by the Spirit into the most thrilling, challenging days in Church history that the world has ever known.

Chapter Two
Spiritual Trends

† God will raise up a new reformation of the Spirit out of the ashes of defeat.

† A new reformation will face critical dissection by theologians and scholars, while the move of God continues among common people who are open to God's voice.

† One tactic Satan will use to delay Kingdom manifestation is to force those moving under the cloud of God to defend their message and their actions.

† Men with messages from God ignite movements which become monuments—religious systems, denominations, organizations.

† The greatest persecution against a new move of God will derive from those who stopped growing spiritually during the last move of God.

† God wants His people to be ready to move continually with His direction for them rather than to rely on established patterns, laws and methods.

† Moving with God involves constant sifting, refining and redefining of goals and specific direction.

† The most painful persecution will cause internal wounds in the body of Christ and will not come from outside sources.

† The Church must cease merely making adjustments to maintain ministries when the visions of those ministries are dead.

† The two roles of prophet and priest will come together for the health of the body of Christ in dealing with sin.

† God will bring judgment *to* the Church and *through* the Church as it becomes a witness and a standard against world systems.

† By the turn of the century, denominations as we know them will no longer exist.

† When the ministries of apostle and prophet return throughout the decade of the 90's, so will the anointed power to judge the Church supernaturally.

† Until the system called *religion* deals with the problem of sin, scandals will surface repeatedly, particularly in Pentecostal and Charismatic circles.

† Christians will learn the difference between ministry that is anointed by God and ministry that is maintained by the flesh.

† God's judgment against the misuse of finances in God's house will continue.

† Ministries that refuse to address financial accountability will be judged by God and will become ineffective.

† Christians will be required to protect the Sabbath day.

† God will bless those who recognize the *elders at the gate* of cities.

† God will purify the worldly language of our children.

† God will continue to judge an infiltration of paganism into the Church as a result of unholy relationships.

† God will designate His priesthood in the modern Church.

2

OUT OF ASHES

Birth of a vision; death of a vision; out of the ashes God raises up His plan. This pattern is repeated so many times in Scripture that it can almost be considered a law in the way God mobilizes His people to action toward the culmination of history.

The visionary himself—Abraham, Moses, Joseph, David, etc.—experiences the entire process in his own life. God calls a man to fulfill an incredible mission, then allows all the things he attempts in his own strength to fail. His own hopes are shattered. In failure and resignation, the visionary is then used to fulfill God's plan, His vision, in a way that the man of God never imagined in the beginning. Like Jacob, all true visionaries walk with a limp, stripped of pride in themselves.

And what are some examples of the historical visionaries of the Church? God chooses a man or a group of men to be His voice proclaiming a particular message of power to a particular generation: for example, Martin Luther's justification by faith, John Wesley's methodism, the Classical Pentecostals' baptism in the Holy Spirit, Oral Roberts' healing by the laying on of hands, Kenneth Hagin's word of faith, and most recently, Kingdom principles demonstrating responsible Christianity as the witness of the empowered Church.

A message from God catches fire and spreads quickly as a life-giving movement. Theologians rush on the heels of the movement to record its disciplines, write its bylaws, critique its intents and purposes and examine its fruit. If the movement has gained enough strength, principles of the movement are studied in seminaries as theological theories. Of course, categorized as one of many theories, the message is analyzed under a microscope and dissected under critical examination. Meanwhile, outside the lab, the fire continues to spread.

Theological analysis eventually calls upon those who are enlightened by the message to defend it. Fear enters the camp. Some defend themselves by going to extremes in stating their case. They begin to give an added punch to the message in some places or soften its sharp edges in others.

In their evaluations of the message and the movement the critics point first to the extreme dangers. Personalities, the characteristics and resumes of the messengers, become the major issue in determining the movement's credibility. The movement becomes a verbal war of debate among the theological elite, an open-ended book war that slows down those following the direction of the Holy Spirit. Critics focus on issues of intellectual argument instead of realizing results from faith in action. Because the leaders are forced to debate defensively, the movement slows down to allow opportunities for explanations.

Usually within one generation a movement becomes a monument, a *form* void of God's power, a system, a denomination. The written bylaws state the terms of belief and judgment. Judgment falls on any spiritual direction other than that which is rigidly designated by the structural boundaries. The most harsh judgment falls upon lawbreakers within the system who (for whatever reason) fall or fail or don't measure up. Scripture teaches, "the letter [law] kills . . ." (2 Corinthians 3:6), but men love rules and regulations—written on the books, rather than upon their hearts.

Soon the system maintains a counterfeit of the genuine move of the Lord. Things look impressive from a distance. Worship, preaching, activities, plans, etc., often look very close to the real thing—God's thing. Churches appoint committees to keep the programs going just to ensure that people stay actively involved. The system survives! Churches do *good* things, but not *God's* things.

When the process begins again—another man proclaims a message from God—the greatest persecution will arise from those who stopped growing spiritually during the last move. They feel that they must defend the truth they received. True messages of God never invalidate the truth of His Word. A move of God only deepens understanding by confirming previous enlightenment, but persecutors are as fixed in their illumination of Scripture as Pharisees. At the same time, they refuse even to acknowledge their own spiritual complacency. They refuse to consider how or why the power of God has left their ministries and their churches.

As long as they are right—and they are sure that they were right during the visitation of the Lord among them twenty (or two hundred) years ago—the goal of ministering under God-anointed power today is not so important. They must continue to hold on to whatever it was God did back then. They are happy where they are, believing the way they do. They are comfortable and safe in all their doctrines. All Christians within their walls are guaranteed that they are going to heaven. What more is there? Oh yes, they teach their children to recite all the right answers to all the right questions.

Then suddenly, God shakes them up. The shaking is called *renewal* or *reformation.* A voice crying out in the wilderness breaks through organizational barriers to reach deaf ears. God allows some ministries to wither away. Some completed visions disintegrate into ashes. Funds are cut off, leaders fall in a variety of ways and sheep become hungry and thirsty for green pastures and cool water. Some people begin remembering how to pray and to seek God's direction again. They agree on one thing—the new wine cannot be contained in old wineskins. The new message is dynamic and will burst old concepts at the seams.

The reformation process is painful and frightening. People make choices during change, good and bad; some get wounded and others get off track in the shuffle. Moving takes much more effort than sitting still. Moving involves risks—especially when the journey is uncertain in its destination and duration. People get tired; they mumble and complain over every decision. The pendulum of direction seems to swing from one extreme to another before balancing with any degree of theological safety in the center. Once again, a vision becomes reality, then it is sifted, refined and redefined. Some Christians—and especially Christian leaders who are themselves sifted, refined and redefined—feel at times as if they will never know peace and joy again.

AN EXAMPLE

Allow me to illustrate with a painful, personal example. In the late 70's, God gave me a vision for raising up a youth army to confront the drug problem at Southwest DeKalb High School in the neighborhood of our church. The direction came as a group of concerned parents, some of them elders in our church, asked for prayer over the lives of their children who were actually participating in the drug traffic. In the days that followed a concentrated prayer session, God showed me a spiritual vision of thousands of young people coming to know Him and challenging Satan's grip on their lives.

The *wheels within a wheel* of that vision became Alpha, a youth meeting with an upbeat band playing music with a Christian message to the rhythm that teens' ears were tuned to hear. Within a few months every Monday night the walls and aisles of our sanctuary were packed with teenagers. My nephew, Duane Swilley, was mightily anointed of the Lord to lead young people to new life in Jesus Christ. Every week the altar calls resulted in hundreds of young people in tears, some responding to the Lord at the first church service they had ever attended.

Alpha's message touched the leaders at that high school and the floodgate opened. Star athletes, homecoming queens, cheerleaders and class officers set the pace for hundreds of kids who respected their leaders' decisions for the Lord. Drastic turnarounds in the lives of these kids were obvious. Former drug dealers became flaming evangelists. Meanwhile, opinions on Alpha became the topic of conversation throughout our community. Soon kids began flocking from other local high schools to check us out!

Within a year of its beginning, youth leaders from other churches were bringing their youth groups to Alpha on Monday nights. Teachers, coaches and parents came to Alpha and asked Duane and me how they could help us. People who had prayed for years for a spiritual revival at Southwest DeKalb High School were overwhelmed with gratitude that God was answering their prayers. Alpha grew by the hundreds as teens prayed for their unsaved friends, and then within days, led those same friends to the Lord.

Alpha spread like fire as persecution from the outside erupted. One pastor of a large church a few miles from us wrote a tract denouncing the baptism in the Holy Spirit as a valid Christian experience. Some youth leaders at other churches were fired over the support they gave to Alpha. We received undeserved press coverage because a young man ran away from a terrible home situation after he was saved at Alpha. His parents blamed us. We were called a cult. School officials received complaints from the school board that parents were calling and asking them to stop our influence over their children—in one case, because we prevented a young girl from committing suicide and her mother was embarrassed. Guess who got the job of giving the final answer to all the complaints? Right! Me!

But persecution from the outside just made Alpha grow stronger. Through the first half of the 80's, we started a discipleship program to ground these new converts in the Word of God. Fellowship groups from Alpha were the first cell groups in our church. Our singles ministry was born to provide time to form relationships at parties in a wholesome environment on Friday nights. Disciples were learning how to minister, teach, counsel and pray with others for God's direction. Everything was working. But then, instead of serving the vision, we began to make the vision serve us.

Although some of the music was mediocre at times and the ministry was somewhat unpolished, God poured out His blessings without measure. We would make mistakes, and God would correct us with a smile. Then we decided to get our *act* together, to be more professional, to break into the big league. And we did. But our success spoiled us from having total dependence on God.

The emphasis of our preparation began to be the clothes we wore, special effects and our musical repertoire. The band built new stage platforms strung with blinking lights. We added a smoke machine and strobe lights. Alpha had its own television program and national conferences in which we *showcased* our ministry from the stage. We told others the steps to take to duplicate our accomplishments. The kids praying in the corners were featured as the *success* of Alpha less and less, and the Spirit of God quietly walked away. Theft became a problem. Audio and video equipment and musical instruments disappeared into thin air.

Many of those first kids who had come to us through Alpha's ministry were now responsible husbands, wives and parents. Numerous young men had become deacons in our church. The firstfruit of Alpha remained and continued to increase. Young men and women enrolled in our School of Biblical Studies. Four young men who came to our church in those early Alpha meetings now serve as pastors on our Presbytery. But though things on the surface looked the same, the undercurrents were turbulent.

A prophetic voice in our ministry gave the word that Alpha would die within a year if certain conditions were not met. That word was fulfilled. Internal discord among us became obvious to the crowds coming to Alpha. The band worked harder than ever to display a successful formula of ministry, but our efforts yielded minimal results. Replacing the spiritual focus was a *stardom mentality*. Young people lost trust in the goals of the ministry. Band members would argue with one another, then walk on stage together to minister. The more that ministry became a production, the less spiritual substance we had to share with anyone.

Painful? Oh, yes! We could have continued making adjustments and changing our ministers and the ministry format, but the vision was no longer alive. In the beginning of the vision, life sprang up everywhere—like springtime in its seasonal splendor. Under an anointing in the flow of a vision, mistakes were covered by the Spirit of the Lord so that fruit was unharmed. Even now the lessons we learned are valuable to the Alpha leadership who continue to work in various areas of the ministry today. But the moment the Spirit of the Lord departed, mistakes meant spiritual death. Why does the Lord depart? What is the correlation between structure and anointing?

SIN IN THE CAMP

When Israel was defeated in battle, Joshua searched for the reasons. Achan had been deceptive. The entire nation was affected by sin in the camp (Joshua 7). The entire Church asks the question of how to handle sin in the camp today. If we believe the media and rumored reports, the Church stands laden with uncovered sin, mistakes, immorality, judgments against one another, lack of repentance and unforgiveness. What do we do to remove sin from among the troops so that we can march under God's anointing again?

In the Old Testament, all defeats and failures were blamed primarily on sin. The solution to problems was to get rid of the sin by getting rid of the sinner—usually by stoning or expulsion. Adam and Eve were thrown out of the garden. Noah's generation was destroyed by a flood. The term *scapegoat* meant that a prophetic eye would find the cause of sin, then the sinner would receive blame, while others could go free. That strategy for dealing with sin is still carried out in some church groups today.

The Old Testament also established the offices of the prophet and the priest as a dual witness to God's will. The role of the prophet was to call attention to sin. Jonah cried out to Nineveh, "Repent!" Elijah charged Ahab, "You have sinned!" Nathan said to David, "You are the man!" Jeremiah wept in the streets to call attention to Israel's sin. The ultimate goal of the Old Testament prophet was to expose the sinner and bring punishment to him.

The role of the priest was to make sacrifices for the sins and failures of people. Once a year the high priest would go into the Holy of Holies. First he would make atonement for his own sins—a step many preachers miss today. Then he offered atonement for the sins of the people. This sacrament established redemption through substitute sacrifices.

These two roles, prophet and priest, are still necessary in the Church of the Lord Jesus Christ. The Church speaks as the voice of the prophet in saying, "Here is sin which causes divorce. Here is sin which allows the drug market to flourish. Here is sin which causes killing in our streets." We enter the house of God knowing that the prophet will put his finger on sin in our lives. Without the proclamation of the root causes of sin through a prophetic voice, the Church fails to minister in strength.

In the New Testament, God calls sinners to repentance and restoration. He says to the woman found in the act of adultery, "Go and sin no more." He says that if we confess our sins, He is faithful and just to forgive us. Then we can pray confidently, "Forgive us our sins, as we forgive those who sin against us." Honestly, I was already the pastor of a church before I could publicly pray, "Father, forgive me of my sins." No one admitted to sinning in the denomination in which I grew up. Sins were always hidden. If a pastor confessed to sin in those days, he immediately lost his pulpit, or he was given such strict punishment that his ministry died. Because we didn't know how to deal with sin, we totally destroyed the provision of the grace of God.

The priests in the Church still make atonement for sin. The priests offer sacramental authority to forgive, absolve and atone. They offer the Lord's table, the confessional, all the sacramental evidences of salvation. They stand as mediators of reconciliation between sinful man and holy God. The confessional, lost to most Protestants at the 16th Century Reformation, is a necessary step in fulfilling the priestly office of absolving men of their sins through Christ. The priest offers hope and renewal.

The contemporary Church has been divided into two camps for centuries. One is the prophetic camp which has cried out against sin with a mighty evangelical voice. The other is the priestly ministry which has preserved the sacramental authority of the Church. Now God is saying clearly to His Church that the time has come to bring His authority from both of these offices together. Both have validity and both are necessary.

God has never been pleased with separation among members of His body. Recent scandals have indeed been judgment falling against that branch of the Church which rails against sin. God is teaching Pentecostals, Charismatics and Fundamentalists to recognize their inability to minister solely through the prophetic voice.

God always judges us by the standard we set for others. Prophetic ministries have spoken so harshly against sin that we have forgotten how much we need God's compassion and grace for beloved sinners within our own houses. We have grown up bombarded with rules and regulations. Our conduct was scrutinized so closely that our own judgments bred hypocrites. We said, "We're all good because this preacher over here is so wrong." We killed a scapegoat when we detected him. We never understood that in God's eyes, all are sinners. God has allowed us to feel the fires of judgment to bring us to an understanding of our need for the role of His priests.

The priestly ministry alone is also insufficient to fulfill the mission which Christ gave to His Church. God never intended for His people to patronize sin. Many times people growing up under a priestly ministry fail to regard biblical standards of morality because forgiveness is so cheap. It's called *cheap grace*. Parishioners can have a good time all week long, go to confessional on Sundays, and never address the need for changes in their conduct.

Each role—priestly and prophetic ministry—without the balance of the other cannot fully minister to people and equip them to be the bride of Christ. Recent events taking place in the Church are the dealings of God, not unrelated coincidences of human weaknesses surfacing. I believe that we have entered a new reformation. We must understand how to administer the sacraments of the Church without losing the prophetic anointing and power of the Holy Spirit.

REASONS FOR JUDGMENT

Judgment begins at the house of God. God is bringing judgment *to* the Church and *through* the Church as it becomes a witness and a standard against world systems. God is moving in this reformation rapidly. Old Testament judgment removed the sin and the sinner. New Testament judgment calls for repentance of the heart. John the Baptist called Jesus the "Lamb of God, who takes away the sin of the world" (John 1:29).

People have trampled underfoot the blood of Jesus Christ by failing to understand sacramental salvation. We have grasped salvation by faith which is glorious. But we have forgotten that Jesus is saying, ". . . Unless you eat the flesh of the Son of Man and drink His blood, you have no life in you . . ." (John 6:53). Jesus said to Peter, "If I do not wash you, you have no part with Me" (John 13:8). The sacraments are much more than symbols. They embody the authority of Christ through the ministry of His Church.

I prophesy that by the turn of the century denominations, as we know them, will no longer exist. God will transcend denominations in the renewal of the apostolic and prophetic ministries to the Church. Laws and disciplines recorded in denominational by-laws will be lifted to a dimension in which the Holy Spirit will be the mighty judge as He was in the ministry of the early Church. We may experience more judgments like that of Ananias and Sapphira (Acts 5:1-11). When the apostle and prophet return throughout the decade of the 90's, so will God's anointed power to judge the Church supernaturally.

Just as God wanted people of the 16th Century to correct many practices that were misrepresenting the ministry of the Church, so we must also correct our thinking today. We must minister under the anointing of the Holy Spirit and also participate in the sacramental presence of Christ through observing the table of the Lord. We need the dual witness of the prophet and the priest. Only that complete witness will ultimately bring judgment to world systems.

We have created an atmosphere of stardom in religion. There is no place for stardom in God's Kingdom. We have done it both in our music and in our pulpits. God is saying, "I will not share My glory." But we have failed to address the source of God's glory. We have simply pushed God's purposes underground as if they didn't exist. In the process, we have given the world a little ball to play with and they have tossed it around. Repeatedly, dilemmas surface with dreadful consequences, and God asks, "Will you listen this time?"

Until the system called *religion* deals with sin, scandals will surface over and over and over again, particularly in Pentecostal and Charismatic circles. When transgressions are committed in the sacramental Church, decisions are made behind the safe confines of monastic walls. They bury their AIDS victims. They deal with infidelities to their vows, and the world is closed out of the process. God's Word has shown us how to do this, as well as how to restore the sinner.

Where sin abounds, grace does much more abound. Jesus said, "Blessed are the merciful, for they shall obtain mercy" (Matthew 5:7). The judgments the Church has imposed upon itself are not God's judgments. We are the ones deciding what is acceptable and unacceptable. We are the ones pointing our fingers at sin and at sinners, yet offering them no solutions. God judges us by our own words. By the same standards that we use to judge others, we are judged.

When King David sinned, he said to his seer, Gad, ". . . Please let us fall into the hand of the Lord, for His mercies are great; but do not let me fall into the hand of man" (2 Samuel 24:14). David knew that people judge rather than forgive. God deals with our sins, and then He restores the sinner.

GOD'S COVERING

A part of our covenant is God's covering of our sins. The blood of Jesus covers us. That is the purpose of the atoning blood of Christ. In covenant, we dwell in the secret place of the Most High. He becomes our covering—not to give us a license to sin, but so we know how to deal with sin when we do fail a test. Under covenant with God we do not judge, we forgive. If we fail to forgive others, God cannot forgive us.

Our judgment toward others yields judgment to us, but mercy toward others grants more mercy to us. We must have the attitude, "But for the grace of God, there go I." Judgment comes when we sow to the flesh; we reap from the flesh. We judge others; therefore, we must be judged by our own standard. We lack mercy, so we cannot receive mercy. We lack forgiveness, and we cannot be forgiven.

By setting our own standards and writing our own disciplines, we have been accused by God just as the Pharisees were accused and exposed by Jesus. Pharisees abound in the Church today. They suffocate God's cause. Because we have never properly understood God's covering to deal with sin privately, we are now judged by the world. Our own words judge us. We write in our bylaws that a man is finished in the ministry if he becomes entangled in a moral problem—whether God is finished with him or not. Or perhaps we write in our bylaws how long he should be on probation from active ministry—ignoring the time frame which God designates for restoration which is a totally individual matter.

God is absolute. Everything that flows from God is absolute. Everything else is relative. Someone asked me the other day if people who smoked cigarettes were going to heaven. I answered, "Just as quickly as those who drink coffee." The nicotine in cigarettes is unhealthy, obviously. But so is the caffeine in coffee. We like to enforce our own moral standards. We say, "You can be a member of our church if you don't drink, don't smoke, and don't go to the local bars." When we fight with one another and turn people in and out of the Church on the basis of our own standards, we make fools of ourselves and of the cause of God.

God is saying that it is time again to address the problems of people who need a new start. God established cities of refuge in the Old Testament (Numbers 35:6). That's the reason we don't turn away the homosexual. We don't turn away anyone trapped in a bad lifestyle. We don't turn away the divorcee. We say, "Here is the house of atonement." In the past I have been castigated for providing an open door to these sinners by some ministers who are now asking me to show them solutions. Solutions are in the heart of God, under His anointing. Solutions are not in writing some new discipline. Solutions are in understanding God's discipline.

REBUILDING THE WALLS

We are indeed on the threshold of the new reformation, but we can stay in the *shaking* for decades unless we let go of the idols which keep us bound to old loyalties. In pride we could have held on to the memories of Alpha's anointed outpouring until this day, but God spoke prophetically, and we let it go. Nehemiah rebuilt the wall surrounding Jerusalem amid great adversity, and we are facing the same spiritual warfare in rebuilding the walls of the Church in this hour. Before reformation, the Church must address specific areas of repentance.

1. The house of God was corrupted by the Spirit of Tobiah (Nehemiah 13:4-8). *This spirit does not know the difference between ministry anointed of*

God and ministry carried on by flesh. Mixture keeps people in constant conflict with one another. Remember, good things are not necessarily God's things. Some departments of a church battle this spirit constantly—especially an outreach ministry where the purity of the message is so essential to fulfilling God's calling, or a worship and arts ministry where so many egos are fighting to be in the spotlight.

God is calling His people to a purity which is almost the same as innocence. In the reformation of God's house, there is no place for ego or self-serving motives to be gratified in the name of ministry. Talent must serve a vision, not a vision serve talent. God will purge impurities from His house. The bride of Christ will be pure.

2. *The treasurers were unfaithful over God's money* (Nehemiah 13:10-12). We have seen God allow the secular world to judge the misuse of finances among people who were given true visions from the Lord. Misuse of finances is one of the major issues of judgment today. Large sums of money corrupt God's people, but we must learn how to use wealth according to God's plan. Don't be foolish enough to think that His plan will not require money—it will!

Mammon is a god who keeps the Church under its power even now. How do we break the bondage? First, we call leadership back to the ministry (verse 11). Ministers are not entertainers. Ministry must serve Jesus, not things, not even projects. The callings of God are without repentance. Leadership must be in place, in the proper structure of God's house. Ministers get into financial problems by moving outside their original callings from the Lord. Headship and structure are essential to God's blessings upon the finances of His house.

3. *The distribution of finances were not according to God's plan* (Nehemiah 13:13). Trust in finances is such an issue in the judgment of the Church today. Will this money go to meet this particular need, or will it buy someone a mink coat and a bigger house? Will money given to God mean advantages to some, while others do not have their needs met?

Ministries that refuse to address financial accountability will be judged by God. The tithe should support the ministry and offerings should support projects. I pray for faithful, trustworthy administration in ministry. One of the greatest areas of battle in the Church today is between pastors and their administrators. These conflicts always hinder the fulfillment of God's purposes in ministry. Again, are finances spent according to God's vision, His plan, or are they spent according to good things, a counterfeit that will never accomplish God's purposes? Do we support a vision, or does the vision support us, our plans and our desires?

4. *The people of God profaned the Sabbath* (Nehemiah 13:14-21). Scripture calls for protection of the Lord's Day, a Holy day set aside to honor the Lord. The Sabbath has become an athletic day, a holiday at the lake or a day to catch up on our work. No! God calls for a day to renew our covenant with Him.

Some point to our society and to the lifestyles we lead as a ready excuse, but attendance to God's house is not an option for a covenant Christian. Inconveniences such as bad weather, guests from out of town, vacations, a special on television, etc., become profane in our lives if they cause us to ignore the Sabbath. I believe that the Church cannot be strong unless we set aside a time of renewal, refreshing, a coming together with God's people to hear from Him that becomes an unbreakable commitment of our hearts. Think of the Sabbath as maintaining a precious relationship with one whom you love.

5. *Spiritual leadership needs to recognize its responsibility for safeguarding the gates of the city* (Nehemiah 13:22). The *elders at the gates* is a biblical concept which is growing in application among responsible Church leaders today. Spiritual elders are the ones responsible for addressing crime in a city. They are the ones who must protect innocent people from harm. Gates represent authority. The time has come for the spiritual elders of a city to take their posts seriously. Certainly, God holds them accountable for His judgment over the spiritual condition of their cities.

If indeed God holds eldership within a city responsible for its welfare and safety, doesn't it make sense that elders from other cities would recognize that authority when they come to minister? I am amazed at the *crusades* coming to Atlanta that ignore the local pastors' leadership. They call for members of churches all over the city to attend, and totally disregard the elders at the gates. I am not offended that I am ignored; but my spirit is grieved at the lack of spiritual comprehension of God's structure. God cannot bless a traveling ministry's disregard for elders who are appointed to guard the gates of each city they enter.

6. *Mixture was most notable in the children's speaking the language of the world* (Nehemiah 13:24). What language are we teaching our children to speak? Advertisements? Rock videos? Violent Saturday morning cartoons? Life and death are in the power of the tongue. Words build our lives in the flesh or in the Spirit because our language is a crea-

tive force for good or evil. Are we teaching our children to build their lives on biblical principles?

Children are our fruit. We can hear ourselves in their words, their attitudes. Before it is too late, we must filter the world out of their language or the Kingdom of God will never be manifested in them. They need words of faith and encouragement to endure testing. They need Kingdom songs to get them through temptations and trials. Adults may not be able to decipher the words of a rapper—but kids sure can! Tune their ears to Kingdom sounds, Kingdom words, Kingdom concepts that will keep them in the mainstream of the new reformation. Reward them for the good things they say! And please, listen to them! Kids are never second-class citizens in the Kingdom of God!

7. *God judged an infiltration of paganism by relationships* (Nehemiah 13:27). Intermarriage with pagan women brought down Solomon's kingdom. *Unequally yoked* always refers to believers entering into covenants with unbelievers. Spiritual mixture always results in weaknesses in fulfilling God's plan.

The Kingdom of God is built in trust. All ministry flows out of relationships. A new reformation will mean new commitments, new relationships, and we must be very careful in joining our spirits to others. Spiritual discernment is vital in the networking of ministries around the world. We will have variety in callings, direction and worship, but we cannot have spiritual mixture.

8. *Reformation means that God makes the assignments of His priesthood* (Nehemiah 13:30). One of the most important aspects of reformation in the Church is the recognition of calling. People need to stay in their assigned places of ministry and give their

hearts fully to the work of the Lord in that area. Ambition, comparisons with others, getting out of God's timing, trying to do someone else's job, or lack of zeal in performing one's own task will defeat God's purposes. God is looking for faithful men and women. Promotion comes on the basis of faithfulness over small tasks. Diligence is essential in doing Kingdom work.

We sing a song at Chapel Hill Harvester Church called *Ain't Got Time to Die*. If we serve God in our work, we anticipate each new day and are too busy to dwell on thoughts that bring death or defeat. If we do our assignments joyfully, God is able to reward our efforts—usually by untold blessings and increasing our responsibilities. I believe that God longs for faithful, diligent leadership. I look for leaders at our church among people whom I see picking up paper off the sidewalk, working to park cars on the parking lots, helping our children cross the street, or assisting people in finding their way around the facilities. These are the people I trust with ministry to people who really need help. Why? They are faithful over small things. They will come through when I really need them!

Men know defeat, but God does not. The cross of Jesus Christ must have seemed to men like a total defeat to God's plan. Even the heavenly host must have marveled that God would turn away from His Son. Jesus became sin for us. He drank the very dregs of the cup of death. Yet defeat and victory are both synonymous with the cross. The defeat belongs to Satan, the victory to Jesus.

Out of ashes, God calls us to a vision of victory. Scripture says that Jesus endured the cross for the joy that was set before Him (Hebrews 12:2). What was that vision, that joy? I can almost see it now, a new reformation joining the prophet and the priest together to restore and strengthen God's people for the Church's finest hour with both freedom and responsibility governing Christians' decisions. All things are made ready for the coming of the Bridegroom. The lamps are trimmed; they have the oil of anointing.

Whatever God wants to shake, I say, "Let the residue fall!" Whatever God wants to die, I say, "Let it die!" Whatever He breathes life into, I say, "Live and glorify your Maker! What can I do to help you to grow?" I pray that we will recognize the fresh anointing of the Lord. I pray that we will put all our strength and prayer power behind whatever God calls into being.

The cloud is moving! The day is new! Move, Church! Let Him lead you to the high place of His Kingdom. Look far and wide from the mountaintop. Feel the freedom. Let the anointing flow over you. Read the laws of the Spirit written upon your heart. You will never again settle for the dark dungeon of judgment or form without power!

Chapter Three
Spiritual Trends

† God has called for healing of the Church, but our greatest warfare continues to be internal wounds.

† The Church's witness is now dim because leaders have allowed their eyes to focus upon darkness—sins, scandals, bad reports.

† Trust in spiritual leadership continues to be a major issue affecting the witness of the Church.

† Accountability to eldership and disciplined lifestyles will be essential to future leadership.

† Impure motives of spiritual leaders adversely affect the witness of the Church.

† The release of a spirit of uncovering will affect the Church first, and then threaten social freedoms and the stability of government.

† The Church will learn to respond in faith in the midst of persecution instead of uncovering others.

† Spirits of uncovering are *light killers.*

† We must cover the sin of one in spiritual authority who speaks some word or commits some deed of the flesh.

† We must protect our strategy whenever some divine mission is at stake.

† Uncovering is necessary whenever spiritual headship is leading sheep into darkness.

† A ministry must be uncovered when there is a hidden agenda or wrong motives in what is represented to be a divine mission.

† The Church is currently undergoing the same tests that Jesus gave to the people in the Judean villages where He walked because we are so close to realizing Kingdom reality in our generation.

† The principle of rejection occurs when people reject God

by rejecting His voice and His move in the earth through the Church.

† Anointed ministries are pressing people to make eternal choices.

† The penalty for rejecting God's anointing is death.

† The true Church must support any cause that is anointed by God as being His cause—in individuals, in ministries, in the policies governing the nations of the earth.

† Satan is trying to bind the Spirit of the Lord, the Strong Man, so that he can plunder God's house.

† The Church must bless relationships that God has joined together.

† The Church must discern between causes that are of God and those which are not.

† The Church must withhold her blessing from those who work against the cause of God.

3

LOVE COVERS

The heathen rage! So, what else is new? Should Christians feel defensive when the media attacks the Church? Should we separate ourselves from association with Christians who are scandalized in sin in order to protect our own reputations? Should we become consumed with planning defensive instead of offensive strategy to counteract the plots against Christianity from secular or political humanists? Absolutely not! Attacks from the outside, from any world system, will never destroy a move of God. God laughs at humanistic plots (Psalm 2:1-4). Our real problems are much closer to home.

Internal strife brings quick destruction. Internal

strife destroys the health of the body. In 1983 I wrote a book called *The Wounded Body of Christ*, one of many books Christian teachers were writing on the theme of forgiveness and unity. I believe since that time the Church has been on the road to recovery. Many ministries of restoration were hearing the same exhortation of the Lord to apply the balm of healing to the Church. God was saying that the time had come for us to open our doors to other Christians for dialogue and understanding.

It has been a rough road, however! As we press toward our high calling to shine the light of Jesus Christ as that witness, that city upon a hill, the greatest attacks, confrontations and defeats continually come from those within our walls who work against the will of the Lord to heal the Church. The devil knows that internal wounds hurt us the most. Many hurt the cause of God and believe that they are serving as channels of healing. They will tell you that God has appointed them to purge others. We still have important lessons to learn—and we must learn them quickly.

With the exception of *Jesus Loves Me,* no song is more associated with the children's ministry of a church than the song, *This Little Light of Mine.* I love to watch the conviction in the eyes of children who love Jesus when they sing, "I'm gonna' let it shine!" But what if the light doesn't shine so brightly? What about the times that the darkness in the Church is so great, so overwhelming, and our witness against the world's darkness seems to be only a flicker?

No one disputes the fact that darkness covers the earth today. National leaders work as international drug dealers. Children stand in the streets and throw rocks at the soldiers who invade their homeland. The numbers of homeless people continue to increase. Children are killed by vicious dogs roaming their neighborhoods. Oppressed people join political revolutions igniting in nations around the globe. Terrorists strike unsuspecting people without warning. We see video tapes of the impassioned pleas of hostages begging their governments to negotiate for their release. Our world is in trouble! And according to the news media, so is the Church. Now, let's get to the root cause of our problems.

> The lamp of the body is the eye. If therefore your eye is good, your whole body will be full of light. But if your eye is bad, your whole body will be full of darkness. If therefore the light that is in you is darkness, how great is that darkness! (Matthew 6:22,23)

What has happened to *the lamp* of the body, the eyes of the Church? When spiritual leaders walk in darkness, the entire body lacks direction. Spiritual leaders are the eyes of the body of Christ in the world. When they are shown publicly as being blinded, the media makes a laughingstock of our message. All the sordid facts concerning fallen leaders unleash a spirit of mockery against Christianity to the ears of those needing most the hope we have to offer. Too often our defense to the world's questions sounds either too simplistic or *spiritualized*. We cover-up instead of simply admitting that as human beings we've made wrong choices with tragic consequences.

What are the lessons? Where do we go from here? When people get off course, a move of God can become no more than unsavory salt fit only to be trodden underfoot or a light to be hidden under a bushel. But the alarms have sounded. The warnings have gone forth. Once correction begins, God will cleanse His temple.

People's trust in spiritual headship is unquestionably the major issue resulting from adverse publicity of fallen leaders. Though the exposure is always shocking, the problems are not new. No one can read the gospels without realizing that Jesus was angry with certain practices of the religious leaders of His day. He called them, "Hypocrites! Thieves! Liars! Vipers!" (Matthew 7:5; 12:34). Why? These leaders had set unreachable standards of living which became heavy burdens upon the people. They stood at the gates of the Kingdom and would not enter, nor allow others to enter either. Religion offered people formulas and practices instead of spiritual solutions from God. Jesus said of their leadership,

> Let them alone. They are blind leaders of the blind. And if the blind leads the blind, both will fall into a ditch. (Matthew 15:14)

Jesus was always angry when supposedly spiritual men could not discern spiritual matters accurately—as God saw them. These leaders did not recognize the visitation of God among them. They knew the Scriptures, but not the reality of scriptural fulfillment. They even prayed with pride by making a display of their spirituality on the street corners.

These religious leaders honored their historical prophets, but rejected the very spirit of prophecy walking their streets and speaking to them (Revelation 19:10). Only dead prophets were credible in their religion. Jesus' ministry was not only rejected as being sent from God, but they also constantly sought for ways to trap Him in His words and actions. The only reason they did not kill Him on the spot was because they feared the great crowds who followed Him.

The gospel of John gives a beautiful metaphor of Jesus as the Light coming into a world of darkness (John 1:6-9). Why was He rejected?

And this is the condemnation, that the light has come into the world, and men loved darkness rather than light, because their deeds were evil. For everyone practicing evil hates the light and does not come to the light, lest his deeds should be exposed. But he who does the truth comes to the light, that his deeds may be clearly seen, that they have been done in God. (John 3:19-21)

When the motives are wrong and the intentions are evil, even those representing the Church have no light to shine in a world of darkness. Ministries try to fool people into accepting their words when their lives do not match up to their message. Such ministry leads people into false security, and ultimately, into deception. Then God must intervene to protect sheep from being led astray. But what is the cause of such darkness in the body of Christ today? How do we fan the fire of true witness? Where do we make corrections?

WHY THE LIGHT IS DIM

First, the light of the Church has become dim due to a lack of self-discipline in leadership. The *stardom mentality* has put ministry in a place in which few men or women of God can survive without clear direction from the Lord. All the trappings of fame and fortune can work to corrupt a spiritual leader's sense of values. Without some spiritual accountability to correct and to cover them, these religious *stars* become as self-destructive as many examples of stars in entertainment. They lose their identities between their public and private worlds. The personal pressures are enormous, so drugs, alcohol or improper relationships become a temporary reprieve from the burden of maintaining *the image* of people's unrealistic expectations.

These leaders are not totally responsible for creating the stardom mentality themselves. People insist on having their heroes. They have made these leaders into *stars,* asking for their autographs, imitating their clothes and hairstyles, buying their records, tapes and posters, and insisting they maintain a Hollywood persona. I know that those caught in the midst of such public expectations are often confused as to how they can survive the spotlight— they know they are not the *image* people insist they become. Such pressure demands great spiritual maturity and accountability—and it's amazing how few of these *stars* are submitted to the spiritual covering and to the counsel of eldership in a local church.

The light of the Church has become dim because the motives of religious leaders are questionable. Numerous houses with extravagant furnishings, expensive cars, furs, jets and high salaries dim the light. Money, the love of which is the root of all evil, takes its toll on the personal integrity of many wealthy leaders and their families in ministry. Good stewardship is a basic principle of Scripture from the beginning of creation. Padded bank accounts from people's contributions to the work of the Lord dim the light of the Church. Questions concerning pastors' lifestyles are inevitable for those of us in the ministry. And why not? Isn't *lifestyle* a major issue of demonstrating the gospel of the Kingdom? Isn't it time that leaders set examples with good stewardship, financial sacrifice and covenant with God?

The light of the Church is dim because brother wars against brother in God's house. Christians are fooling themselves if they believe they can witness to an unsaved world and yet separate themselves from fellowship with those born of the same Holy Spirit in the body of Christ. Judgmentalism has released the spirit of judgment in the lives of those who rail against others. Meanwhile, the world looks on in dismay. They ask, "How can a fragmented Church possibly have answers for my problems?"

Finally, the light of the Church is dim because of a spirit of uncovering. The consequences of uncovering the sins of others are often ignored among Christians who believe that they have been divinely appointed by God to purge the Church. Scripture proves destructive consequences for one assuming that role. The one who uncovers always becomes enslaved.

> And Noah began to be a farmer, and he planted a vineyard. Then he drank of the wine and was drunk, and became uncovered in his tent. And Ham, the father of Canaan, saw the nakedness of his father, and told his two brothers outside. But Shem and Japheth took a garment, laid it on both their shoulders, and went backward and covered the nakedness of their father. Their faces were turned away, and they did not see their father's nakedness. So Noah awoke from his wine, and knew what his younger son had done to him. Then he said: "Cursed be Canaan; a servant of servants he shall be to his brethren." (Genesis 9:20-25)

The story of Ham's looking upon his father's

nakedness is the classic story of uncovering (Genesis 9:18-24). No one can excuse Noah's drunkenness, his nakedness, nor his shameful example of behavior before his sons. But the story is more about a curse upon Ham for uncovering his father than it is a story intended to expose Noah's sin. Regardless of his behavior, Noah was still a spiritual elder, chosen of God—right or wrong in his actions. Ham's descendants inherited the consequences of his uncovering the man of God.

During the past few years we have witnessed uncovering at every level of Church, government and business. Trust has become a major issue of political campaigns. Few public leaders are left unscathed. Under close scrutiny, every leader, his family and his distant relatives have collected tarnish somewhere! When the spirit of uncovering is rampant in a society, no one is perceived as trustworthy. Past mistakes become a more important criterion for eliminating leaders than their ability to do a certain job. Suspicion clouds our perceptions and makes us question everyone's actions or any reports we receive. A person's word is regarded as being irrelevant. Everyone must offer tangible proof for anything he says.

I charge the Church with opening the door to a spirit of uncovering which now permeates society. Some self-proclaimed inspectors took out a magnifying glass and began accusing spiritual leaders of seduction. They called true visions of God *visualization*. They attacked Christian counseling as being grounded in sorcery—though some of the attackers needed counseling desperately themselves. They hired private detectives to follow Christian leaders around in an attempt to catch them in questionable circumstances and expose them. And the world laughed at the Church's dirty laundry while they, too, fell under the power of the spirit of uncovering.

Unless the flame of the Church ignites with the light of compassion and forgiveness of sins, within two decades spirits of judgment and uncovering will destroy the freedom we enjoy in America. This same spirit became an avalanche leading to government takeovers in Russia and Cuba. Russian churches became objects of inspection. Revolution against weaknesses in the Church was quickly followed by revolution against the heads of government. One day the police were knocking on the doors of churches, and the next day private citizens were under investigation and ordered to reveal every detail of their private lives. Mistrust of leadership and instability of a society go hand in hand. In an unstable system, one spark sets off a revolution that topples any semblance of freedom.

Please understand that I am making no room for justifying evil in the house of God! Christians are called to righteousness and holiness, and high standards of conduct are especially vital for teachers of God's Word. I am reminding the Church that we, ourselves, have opened the door, uncovered our sins and allowed the world to judge us. We have been irresponsible in flaunting weaknesses which should have been addressed within the confines of the Christian community. We have started down a path which could lead our nation, the stronghold of freedom in the world, to anarchy and collapse. The spirit of uncovering will lead us quickly to a life of servitude in work camps.

This is the message which we have heard from Him and declare to you, that God is light and in Him is no darkness at all. If we say that we have fellowship with Him, and walk in darkness, we lie and do not practice the truth. But if we walk in the light as He is in the light, we have fellowship with one another, and the blood of Jesus Christ His Son cleanses us from all sin. (1 John 1:5-7)

Spiritual light is much more than symbolism in God's Word. The Day of Pentecost is always associated with tongues of fire resting upon the heads of those praying in that upper room. Isn't that an interesting detail of that monumental event? Light upon their heads speaks of enlightenment as well as light shining in a dark world. When enlightenment ceases, darkness fills the body. And yet we have allowed *teachers* to equate genuine enlightenment, illumination and revelation of the Holy Spirit with spiritual seduction. Destructive persecution always comes from the inside. Outside persecution usually strengthens the Church, but internal persecution always weakens it. The eyes become darkened and the body is filled with darkness.

People of light always respond with faith in the midst of persecution instead of reacting by uncovering others. For example, Joseph sat in prison unjustly accused of a crime. Never once did Joseph uncover Potiphar's wife by suggesting that his master find out how many men his wife had been with previously. Joseph simply sat in prison until the chief butler to Pharaoh remembered the young Hebrew's gift of interpreting dreams (Genesis 41:9-13). Now that is an example of faith in the sovereignty of God! Joseph knew who was in charge.

The Church is presently experiencing a reaction to darkness instead of heeding a call to repentance from sins that dim our light. We are still reacting to putrid things we have seen in the search light rather than realizing our mission by shining the light of Christ against the world's darkness. Character is formed under pressure. Some people have reacted to recent scandals by saying, "I told you so!" "All preachers are hypocrites who are only interested in money!" "Good enough for them! They deserve it!" Such outbursts grieve the Spirit of the Lord.

Spirits of uncovering are *light killers*. This spirit is evident in Adam's reaction to God when he was questioned about his sin. Adam defended himself by saying, "The woman whom You gave to be with me . . ." (Genesis 3:12). In uncovering Eve, Adam uncovered himself.

Absalom is an example of uncovering David who was not only his father, but who was also the king of Israel. He stood at the gate and uncovered the weaknesses in his father's authority. He instigated mistrust against his father's administration and misappropriated the people's trust to himself. Why was Absalom killed? He was killed for speaking against headship (2 Samuel 15).

Vashti, the queen, uncovered the lack of the king's authority over her by refusing his request to attend his banquet. She made her own banquet for the women. The king was reminded by his advisors that her actions set a precedent for other women in the kingdom. A spirit of uncovering had been released, and other women would follow the queen's example in uncovering their own husbands. The king had no choice but to send her away (Esther 1:19).

The spirit of uncovering is not the same as closing our eyes to the sins and weaknesses of others. We must never ignore error by pretending it doesn't exist. The eye is the light of the body. The leadership of the Church must be aware and responsive to places where correction is needed in order to maintain health and strength.

WHEN TO COVER

So what do we do when we know that sins and weaknesses exist in the lives of those around us? I have already written concerning the need for the confessional and the ministry of the priest to hear a sinner's confession and assure his forgiveness of sin. The combined ministries of priest and prophet provide the proper structure to deal with sin. Let me emphasize again that all have sinned and need cleansing daily—including leadership in the body of Christ. I will address in the next chapter the proper place of the confessional of those in the ministry. New wineskins, new structure, is one of the greatest reforms taking place in the Church today.

Love covers (1 Peter 4:8). There are three times when we must cover the sins we recognize in others for the protection of the body of Christ and for God's will to be served. *First, we always cover the sin of one in spiritual authority who speaks some word or commits some deed of the flesh.* Mature Christians always realize that the Holy Spirit is housed in earthen vessels. The fruit of the Holy Spirit may be beautiful in a person, but that person's flesh will always be flesh as long as that God-called, Spirit-filled minister is alive. He/she will have good days and bad days. He/she will have moods and reactions to stressful situations that are not exemplary spiritual responses.

Many Christians do not want to admit that everyone is a sinner and falls short of God's glory— especially when the sinners are their spiritual leaders. The fact remains that even the most beautiful Christian needs cleansing daily by the blood of Christ.

God made provisions for the cleansing of His priests before they offered sacrifices for people's sins. Our greatest efforts to attain righteousness are called *filthy rags* in Scripture (Isaiah 64:6). Christians fall into pharisaical deception whenever they regard the vessel as more than housing for the treasure of the Holy Spirit. Our only righteousness is the righteousness of Christ within us.

The realization that flesh is flesh should prompt covering of God's ministers whenever that flesh is exposed. Ham uncovered God's spokesman by exposing Noah's flesh. Perhaps he felt justified in his own mind. Noah was wrong to lie around drunk. But Ham's reaction became more of an issue with God than Noah's drunkenness. Noah's sin was flesh; Ham committed a sin against the Spirit of God when he touched the one whom God had called. Ham mocked God's spokesman and bore the penalty of a profane spirit.

The second reason to cover for the protection of the Church is when a divine mission is at stake. Rahab, the harlot, protected the spies of Israel and deliberately sent the men of Jericho on a wild goose chase after them (Joshua 2:1-24). It's interesting that she hung a scarlet cord in the window as a sign to the spies (verse 21).

That scarlet cord covered God's mission—an act which the mind of reason would call a sinful, deceptive lie. If pharisaical minds could get past the fact that Rahab was a harlot whom God used in His mission, they would still condemn her for lying. God honors her. Rahab is listed with other great men and women of faith who have served in obedience to God as role models for the Church (Hebrews 11:31).

When a divine mission is at stake, giving public

75

answers and explanations is not a wise course to take. Silence becomes appropriate. God will protect His people from danger if they are participating in a divine mission, following the guidance of the Holy Spirit and acting in faith. Scripture provides numerous examples of covering to protect God's mission. Joseph covered Mary's extraordinary pregnancy. Undoubtedly, people asked questions about the couple's morals and the circumstances of Mary's pregnancy. The Apostle Paul escaped Jewish persecution in Damascus by being dropped down the city wall in a basket—hardly a dignified exit for a man of God (Acts 9:23-25). Today we would hear this story and someone would inevitably ask, "Why wouldn't God supernaturally protect His apostle as He did at other times?" God used spiritual men to cover Paul. A healthy body protects its members.

Finally, covering is necessary for the protection of the Church when exposure would destroy the faith of innocent people. James contends that true and undefiled religion is to care for orphans and widows in their trouble and to keep unspotted by the world (James 1:27). Eldership in the body of Christ is so important in these matters. They must ask themselves whether exposing the facts would better serve innocent people than covering the facts for the protection of others. They must sometimes decide who needs to know the details of a matter, and who needs to be covered. The one against whom an offense is committed usually needs to hear the confession—but other people do not need to know nor do they need to hear it.

For example, a pastor should cover a young man who admits to his pastor that he struggles against the temptations of homosexuality. The person who is the object of temptation may need to know, but no one else. Even that young man's family does not need to know of his spiritual battles in that area. Innocent people would be hurt by such a disclosure—as in the case of the young man's wife and children. Other relationships—friendships, for example—could be negatively affected without just cause. His job could also be affected by such a disclosure.

Or perhaps an associate pastor confesses to a senior pastor that he has misappropriated funds. If the situation can be resolved without public exposure, that associate pastor need not miss one step in the ministry. He could realize his weaknesses in that area, repent, resolve the issue by exercising appropriate accountability in the future and go on. If the senior pastor realizes that his associate has an unresolved spiritual problem and cannot be trusted, perhaps that pastor needs to leave the ministry. If so, he can leave in good standing instead of scandal because covering is provided for him. God will honor spiritual covering both in that ministry and in the life of the one who is released to do other work.

WHEN TO UNCOVER

I can imagine the questions in readers' minds. When does *covering* become *cover-up?* The matter of spiritual covering demands great spiritual maturity. Sometimes a fine line separates covering and cover-up, and no two situations are to be regarded as the same. Many times the greatest gauge for determining covering is the spiritual attitude of the one who has committed sin. Is repentance genuine? Is there a desire for restitution and restoration? What are the issues at stake? Who are the people whose lives are at stake? Sometimes a trial period of covering is necessary in order to answer those questions adequately and appropriately. If the attitude toward sin is not one of repentance, when should a matter be uncovered?

Uncovering is necessary when spiritual headship is leading sheep into darkness. Jesus warned of deception in the last days. Correction for headship must always come from those over them in the Lord—not from the sheep. God sent His prophet Nathan to confront David with his sin. God always has the proper structure through which to correct His leaders because the welfare of innocent lambs is so vital to God's purposes.

Christians who are unable to name the headship over them are in serious trouble spiritually. We see the devastating results of such lack of structure, accountability and covering in many of the current scandals that the Church is facing. Sheep were being led into darkness because of unconfessed sin and deception, and God allowed the uncovering. Within proper structure, much of the devastation we see in these ministries and the lives of these ministers could have been avoided.

A ministry must be uncovered when there is a hidden agenda or a wrong motive in what is represented as a divine mission. Most people could give examples of ministries that once flowed in spiritual anointing which became nothing more than ego trips. Money began to be used selfishly instead of providing ministry to the needs of God's people. Instead of serving the Lord in ministry, those ministries began to serve their leaders.

I have already discussed the dangers of the *stardom mentality* overtaking those who have been trusted with genuine visions of God. Sometimes people create a ministry environment simply to serve their own needs for power, position and recognition. Although the initial stages of such endeavors may appear promising, God will never bless those missions because improper motives will always surface. For the sake of the sheep, improper motives must be uncovered.

Finally, uncovering is necessary when the innocent stand to lose. God will not allow a prostitution of His mission nor His message. God is longsuffering and will allow periods of grace and correction for individuals, but He will always end abuse in ministry because He is searching for a true witness, a true light. Joseph was silent for thirteen years concerning the abuse of His brothers selling him, but retribution of their wrongdoing against him eventually fell into Joseph's own hands. Whenever innocent people wait upon the Lord to avenge them of unjust treatment, God will repay. Wrongdoing will eventually be uncovered.

But wait! What was Joseph's response when the moment of retribution against his brothers finally arrived? Joseph wept over them. This story expresses the spiritual response God asks of us toward those from whom we have suffered injustices. Jesus' forgiveness of His enemies while He hung on the cross demonstrates the ultimate example for us of a godly response to the injustices we suffer. When God uncovers sin, mature Christians must be spiritually prepared with a response that will bring honor to the Lord and health to the body. Uncovering sin is for the purpose of healing and restoring—we must never forget that goal. Gloating over uncovering is never, never the Spirit of Christ.

THE PRINCIPLE OF REJECTION

The issues of covering and uncovering are especially important for the Church in this hour because we are walking very close to realizing Kingdom reality in our generation. The message of the gospel of the Kingdom is the *gravitational word* the Holy Spirit is speaking to the body of Christ. As when Jesus walked the earth, proclamation of God's rule unleashes unparalleled opportunities as well as conflicts. When the Spirit of the Lord moves, earthly matter is always shaken. Temptations abound and steadily increase as opportunities for ministry increase. Kingdom against kingdom confrontations test spiritual maturity.

What is the test of spiritual maturity today? The Church is currently undergoing the same tests that Jesus gave to the people in those Judean villages where He walked. First, Jesus proclaimed His platform, His mission (Luke 4:16-21; Matthew 5). Then He called definable leaders and gave them assignments (Luke 10:1-11). Finally, He rode into Jerusalem as the King of kings and Lord of lords (Matthew 21:6-11).

After Jesus rode into town as a king, His first act was cleansing the temple (Matthew 21:12). No one can dispute the spiritual purging of God's house today. The proclamation of Jesus' identity as the Son of David immediately drew fire from the chief priests and scribes (Matthew 21:14-16). Any genuine move of the Holy Spirit will surface criticism in those religious leaders opposing God's mission. Finally, Jesus declared that the rule of God would extend as a worldview of His Kingdom authority to all men who received His message (Matthew 21:43-46). Today mass communication has given us unparalleled opportunity to take the gospel of the Kingdom to all people and to disciple all nations.

God is using the principles of rejection to test the Church in this hour. What is this principle?

> He who receives you receives Me, and he who receives Me receives Him who sent Me. He who receives a prophet in the name of a prophet shall receive a prophet's reward. And he who receives a righteous man in the name of a righteous man shall receive a righteous man's reward. And whoever gives one of these little ones only a cup of cold water in the name of a disciple, assuredly, I say to you, he shall by no means lose his reward. (Matthew 10:40-42)

Today men are rejecting God wherever they reject an anointed move of God. God is using this principle of rejection not only to confront those who are closed to hearing His voice, but also to find people with spiritual vision and hope. Today some people are crying out, "Hosanna! Blessed is He who comes in the name of the Lord!" They may not understand all the theology, disciplines, doctrines or dogma, but they know when they have experienced a genuine encounter with God. Within the house of God, eternal choices are being made. Anointed ministries are pressing people to make those choices.

> I do not pray for these alone, but also for those who will believe in Me through their word; that they all may be one, as You, Father, are in Me, and I in You; that they also may be one in Us, that the world may believe that You sent Me. And the glory which You gave Me I have given them, that they may be one just as We are one: I in them, and You in Me; that they may be made perfect in one, and that the world may know that You have sent Me, and have loved them as You have loved Me. Father,

I desire that they also whom You gave Me may be with Me where I am, that they may behold My glory which You have given Me; for You loved Me before the foundation of the world. O righteous Father! The world has not known You, but I have known You; and these have known that You sent Me. And I have declared to them Your name, and will declare it, that the love with which You loved Me may be in them, and I in them. (John 17:20-26)

Jesus' prayer here gives more intimate insight into His heartfelt love for the Church than any other words in Scripture. No wonder the warfare among Christians rages so. No wonder our light is dimmed by controversy as Satan attacks the eyes of the body of Christ. Darkness floods the body when we uncover one another's sins and expose one another's weaknesses for the world to see instead of demonstrating the love of Christ. Such actions directly oppose God's plans and purposes for His Church.

When we follow the leading of the Holy Spirit, we are joined to Christ in an inseparable relationship. In that relationship with Christ, we actually become standards of judgment upon others who reject His anointing through the witness of our lives and ministries. Our words become life or death to those who receive or reject our message. I know such an understanding can lead to spiritual pride, but I also know that God humbles the proud quickly when so much is at stake in His mission.

Samuel prophesied as God's spokesman to Israel. When Israel wanted a king, Samuel became troubled at their request:

Then all the elders of Israel gathered together and came to Samuel at Ramah, and said to him, "Look, you are old, and your sons do not walk in your ways. Now make for us a king to judge us like all the nations." But the thing displeased Samuel when they said, "Give us a king to judge us." So Samuel prayed to the Lord. And the Lord said to Samuel, "Heed the voice of the people in all that they say to you; for they have not rejected you, but they have rejected Me, that I should not reign over them. According to all the works which they have done since the day that I brought them up out of Egypt, even to this day—with which they have forsaken Me and served other gods—so they are doing to you also. Now therefore, heed their voice. However, you shall solemnly forewarn them, and show them the behavior of the king who will reign over them." (1 Samuel 8:4-9)

God told His prophet that the people were rejecting Him by rejecting Samuel's warnings. Today men and women speaking in the Spirit of Christ are facing rejection from those bound by religious traditions and theological intellectualism. Those under the power of the principle of rejection will never acknowledge spiritual healings, signs and wonders, the ministry of contemporary apostles and prophets nor the new reformation of the Holy Spirit sweeping across the earth today. Often those under the power of rejection are not hostile to God, they are merely indifferent to the anointing of the Holy Spirit. Their indifference brings spiritual death.

In the purging of God's house, Christians mature quickly if they respond to the chastening of the Lord. We need not review the same lessons over and over again because we repeatedly fail the same tests. The time has come for us to pass the tests. God is bringing us to minister with a mature love, a love that covers whatever needs to be covered, a love that sees as God sees.

The Spirit of the Lord is moving offensively today, and we must get into the flow and move under the anointing of the Lord to accomplish the tasks at hand. God is now bringing His Kingdom rule to individual hearts. We have seen the beginning of the reign of Kingdom authority in righteous purging of the body of Christ. Finally, God will judge the nations of the earth. Therefore, we must support any cause that is anointed by God as His cause—in individuals, in ministry, in the policies governing the nations of the earth. God's Word is always the final standard by which to judge in any matter.

I was in Washington, D.C. in March 1986 when God spoke to me about Christians praying a prayer of faith releasing His Spirit at state and national capitols. We prayed, "Let My Spirit Go!" at government sites all over the world on July 4th of that year. Recently the Lord gave me further insight into releasing the Holy Spirit to accomplish Kingdom purposes on earth.

> No one can enter a strong man's house and plunder his goods, unless he first binds the strong man, and then he will plunder his house. (Mark 3:27)

Perhaps you have believed as I did that Satan is the strong man to be bound. I have prayed that way for years. Now I understand that Satan tries to bind the Spirit of the Lord so that the devil is free to plunder the house of God. We have experienced Satan's plundering in recent days, but the Lord is calling us to release His Spirit, the Strong Man, to carry out God's will and protect His house. Rejection binds the Lord's work. When the Spirit of God is bound from His house, we have no protection from the enemy. We become fair game at the hands of world

84

systems to plunder us.

We must do no harm to whatever God joins together. God is joining ministries and personal relationships to accomplish His purposes today. Allow me to point out several ways that we reject a move of the Holy Spirit and bind Him from the house of the Lord. One way we can cause delay in manifesting the Kingdom of God is to keep spiritual relationships on the defensive. Anywhere God is doing something that is making a difference, people will stand on the sidelines and criticize those doing the work. One of the easiest ways to destroy God's work is to invalidate the spiritual credentials of those carrying out His assignments. Break unity in the ranks. Break confidence and trust between those whom God has joined together.

We must not patronize those critical spirits, nor can we take the time to answer them. They do not want answers; they want destruction. They are a diversionary tactic of Satan. Jesus prayed, "Father, make them one . . ." Critical spirits will always despise true spiritual unity that accomplishes God's will and manifests His witness to the world.

Gossip, accusations and suspicion are all forces which bind the Spirit of God from accomplishing God's purposes. These spirits are plundering God's house today. They have gained strength through the recent scandals that alert people to focus upon the sins of others. These spirits are spiritual death to God's house. We must wake up to this tactic of the enemy, and bless and protect relationships that are bearing spiritual fruit for the Kingdom of God.

Another way we bind the Holy Spirit from God's house is failing to discern the difference between good and evil. We can be guilty of binding missions of God by calling them missions of the devil. Not only is this spiritual death in God's house, but it becomes blasphemous toward God's will. I fear for those who are calling men of God *heretics*. They are opening themselves to spiritual death.

I believe that many critics of ministries, especially investigative reporters, are moving very close to blasphemy by calling ministries and messages from God to task. While they feel totally justified in their own minds, they are touching God's anointed messengers and His movement throughout the Church. As with the Ark of the Covenant, they cannot touch anointed things and live. Perhaps they will not die naturally, but spiritual death is far worse.

We are responsible to God to pour water on any cause which He begins. We need to nourish it, protect it and support it. This commitment is necessary if we are moving where God is going in the next few years. We must be able to recognize Jesus in those whom we feed, clothe, visit and help (Matthew 25:31-46). We will be judged by our willingness to support the cause of God and by our help to God's people. We must ask, "Where is the anointing of God flowing?" Then we give all our energy, talent, resources and support to that place.

Finally, we bind the Spirit of the Lord from God's house whenever we give any support or credibility to one who is working against God's cause. Satan is subtle in the ways he traps us into doing this. For example, perhaps we bless politicians who promise to work for some of the goals which would be good for our cities. That politician may be mixed in his motives. He might care little for the welfare of citizens and could even be hostile toward the message of the Church.

Perhaps we support and bless ministries that war with others in the body of Christ. We must be careful where we plant seed, financial contributions, in ministry. God holds us accountable to plant seed in good soil so that He can bless it.

We must do all that we can to release the Holy Spirit. God is saying, "Let My Spirit Go!" God needs trustworthy Christians who are dedicated to making ministries secure and sound in what they say and do. Security comes only in following the leading of the Holy Spirit. That is not the same as *playing it safe.* Many times the Holy Spirit prompts us to walk some very risky paths, but we will have confidence and peace whenever we follow the leading of the Lord.

Satan's plundering of God's house must end. The eyes of the body will be filled with light when we stop looking for sin and guilt in other Christians and begin looking to Jesus, the author and finisher of our faith. We must learn when to cover others to protect God's cause, and when God allows uncovering for the healing and restoration of His body. God has sounded the trumpet to individuals; now He is cleansing the temple. The wine is being poured into new wineskins.

We are being prepared as a bride for the Bridegroom, but we are not ready for the wedding yet. Preparation necessitates the release of the Holy Spirit to do His work within us, within the body of Christ, and within the nations of the earth. We've engaged in a few serious skirmishes, but the real battle is still ahead. Until we submit to the rule of God's Kingdom in our own minds and hearts, in our relationships with Christians in our own churches and in other churches, we can hardly tackle the confrontations concerning the rule of God's Kingdom over godless nations. After we pass the tests in elementary school, we can move on with mature understanding, loving actions and Kingdom authority!

Chapter Four
Spiritual Trends

† A Christian's qualities of abundant living will become
more of a contrast to the lives of people practicing legalistic religion or those living without salvation and reconciliation to God.

† The lessons Christians learned in the classical Pentecostal and the Charismatic Movements will be valuable
preparation for the next move of God.

† Satan will try to delay the fresh anointing of the Holy
Spririt by making Christians focus on movements of the
past; to revive them, to relive them or to reconstruct
them.

† The Kingdom message will be *the message* propelling
the Church into the twenty-first century.

† The media will continue to expose Christian scandals in
an attempt to destroy the Church's credibility.

† We are approaching the greatest hour of the ministry of
the local church.

† The strength of anointing of parachurch ministries will
diminish unless they relate their goals directly into
strengthening the work of local churches.

† Singleness of direction and purpose in the universal
Church will become the primary goal of outreach
ministries.

† Traveling ministries will recognize the necessity of their
own covering by elders in a local church in order to
maintain effective ministry.

† Local pastors will rise to the responsibility of their position as gatekeepers and watchmen over their cities.

† Christian ecumenical councils in cities will become
strong by standing together as intercessors and as
spokesmen for quality living.

† Christians will realize that their greatest source of help in any circumstance is their local church.

† Gifts of the Holy Spirit will be identified less with individuals in specialized ministries and more with the ministry of pastors in local churches.

† God will confirm His authority and anointing in particular ministries through physical and emotional health among His people.

† One of the greatest challenges of the next decade will be the scriptural integrity of handling church affairs instead of adopting secular solutions for directing a ministry.

† Finally the Church is learning that *fitly joined together* is the key to becoming the empowered witness.

† The Church will begin to follow the *confess up; minister down* principle of structure, solving many problems of misplaced confidence and its consequences in the ministry.

† Abuses of truth such as what happened in the Shepherding Movement will provide valuable lessons in the formation of new wineskins.

† Meetings providing opportunities for pastors at the same level of ministry to come together will be valuable in maintaining proper structure and covering at every level of responsibility.

† God will determine His future leaders on the basis of their attitudes as students until He calls them to run in the race as teachers.

† God will prepare a new dwelling place for Himself in the new wineskins of the Church.

† In proper positioning, God will be able to trust the Church with the promise of granting whatsoever we ask of Him because we will never violate His holiness, His plan and His will.

4

NEW WINESKINS

Often new ideas scare people in Christian circles for good reasons. But sometimes people are alarmed because they want to protect their own interests. Jesus reminded the leaders of His day that new wine burst old wineskins (Matthew 9:17). His words were not welcome news. *Wineskins* in this context represented the structure of religion—both old and new. The Church was born out of old wineskins (Judaism) with an effervescent quality of spiritual life through the anointing of the Holy Spirit. Jesus came to give us abundant life—a radically different way to look, talk and live when compared to people practicing a legalistic religion or those living without salvation and reconciliation to God.

Abundant living connotes movement, growth, energy, purpose, passion, challenge, excitement, joy, productivity, learning, creative solutions, wholesome relationships and fresh understanding. I know these characteristics are rarely seen in people in the world (past their youth!), but do they describe the lives of average, middle-aged church members sitting in most churches today? A Christian's zeal for living should be notably obvious to everyone he meets. He is *light* in darkness and *salt* in an unsavory environment. He should be a life-giver to people in the most hopeless situations.

Christians proceed from abundant living in this world to eternal assignments at other dimensions of Kingdom living in the heavenly realm when their course is finished here. When people stop growing, they merely exist. They finish living long before they die physically—and there is no greater tragedy. God is the author of creativity and life. Working in His harvest to accomplish His purposes never becomes dull, commonplace or routine.

Church history records the bursting of old wineskins repeatedly. Why? When Church structure begins to suppress God's life-giving power in Spirit and truth, God will find men and women of covenant who will agree with Him for His will to burst forth on earth. God's Word declares that He will do a *new thing;* He makes all things new (2 Corinthians 5:17).

Fresh insights from God, spiritual illumination of His recorded Word, break forth in Christians who seek God's direction with all their hearts. When God does a *new thing,* spiritual life bursts old structures at the seams. Does this mean God changes? No, God's character is absolute and unchanging. His purposes for mankind are also unchanging. God's plan in history, however, unfolds progressively in each generation according to the obedience and faith of Christians living in some designated period of human history.

God is more interested in construction than reconstruction. Christians need to ask, "Where is the Spirit of the Lord actively building in the Church today? What are the projects (ministries) God has called, established and anointed in this day?" Some Christians are sleeping and never even consider those questions. They merely *practice* their faith as their fathers and their grandfathers before them did. One of the greatest challenges of this present day is waking the sleeping giant, the Church.

Some Christian teachers continue traveling in a circular path. They travel repeatedly around the same theological mountain in an attempt to find the place of God's anointing, His power, His message of direction. All the time God is moving sovereignly in a trajectory through human history toward His plan for the culmination of the ages. God has ordained the final scene of human history as manifesting the Kingdom of God in its fullness at the coming of Jesus Christ.

MOVE WITH THE CLOUD

God moves precept upon precept, line upon line, here a little, there a little (Isaiah 28:13). The Holy Spirit always leads us forward, adding to the things we have already learned and never wasting one step of the journey. At times we find ourselves camping out somewhere in the wilderness to review hard lessons before we can move on. Some people inevitably decide to build permanent homes along the way and simply stop moving with the cloud of the Lord. Most present-day denominations began as new wineskins containing a fresh understanding of God's Word and His will. Many of them, however, stopped moving long ago.

The classical Pentecostal Movement and the Charismatic Movement were indisputably releases of the Holy Spirit in fresh anointing upon the body of Christ. At the turn of the twentieth century, Pentecostals opened the total Church to a new understanding of ministry to people's personal needs. Though initially rejected by mainline Protestants and Catholics, the experience of the baptism of the Holy Spirit opened the ministry of spiritual gifts to the body of Christ. Gifts such as healing and deliverance brought the Church into a ministry of body life in which individual members of the body were healed and set free to do the work of the Lord and to live abundantly.

The Charismatic Movement broadened the base of ministering through spiritual gifts by transcending denominational boundaries. In the process God began addressing spiritual bondage that had infiltrated through the holiness disciplines of Pentecostals. Strict codes of dress and other traditions which were more culturally enforced than scripturally based were no longer able to strangle the move of the Holy Spirit. God wanted enlightened Pentecostals to seek Him with righteous hearts and renewed minds, conformed to the righteousness of Christ within them instead of feeling justified before God by outwardly conforming to strict Church disciplines.

Both the classical Pentecostal and Charismatic Movements were preparation for the move of the Holy Spirit in this hour. The illumination of Reformed

Theology is now merging with Pentecostal authority and fire. History is a great teacher. Although understanding the things God has taught us in the past is very important, history must never become our focus for ministry today. Why? The Spirit of God is moving again!

Dwelling on past victories closes people off from the application of God's anointed Word for today—the same error so obvious in the blindness of the scribes and Pharisees of Jesus' day. Now we must address the *new wineskins,* the structure of spiritual authority and callings of the fivefold ministry in the Church of the twenty-first century.

Recently I read an article written by Charles Simpson in the premiere issue of *Christian Conquest* (January/February 1987) which addresses the trends of the past few decades in the spiritual trajectory of the contemporary Church. Charles Simpson writes:

"I have never believed that a new revelation from the Lord means He is annulling the former ones. In fact, fresh revelation helps us to see the past even more clearly. Conversion, spiritual power, Kingdom, and action flow into the next thing that God will say.

"The 1960's were times when *experience* was emphasized. *Existential* and *charismatic* were big words. In the 1970's, *teaching* was emphasized. Many people began turning from introspection toward goals.

"In the 1980's, *action* has become the focus. Both inside and outside the Church, people are being forced out of passivity to act on their convictions. Someone said, 'Heroes are not born; they are cornered.' Christians are being cornered by growing issues and real challenges. It's time to act.

"In the 1990's, world evangelization with the Kingdom message will be the focus. Among many Christians, it already is the focus. This new evangelism will be a message that does more than 'snatch a soul from hell.' It will be a message that the kingdoms of this world shall become the Kingdom of our Christ, and He shall reign forever.

"If we are to move toward God's purpose, we must use what we learned in the 1960's and 1970's, and act now. We must win the battle in the arena of personal and church life so that we can win in the arena of world history."

I revere the heritage of godly forefathers who paid the price of persecution and hardship in seeking the Lord. I honor their obedience to God's direction and their adherence to their assignments from God. We must learn well the lessons they can teach us. In my judgment, however, we only move in circles when we focus upon the significance of past movements in order to reconstruct them, to revive them, or to relive them. This exercise can even become a delay tactic of Satan to miss the fresh anointing of the Holy Spirit at a given hour! Satan will attempt to bind the Strong Man (the Holy Spirit) in order to plunder God's house. Satan's goal is destruction by bringing confusion, mixture, doubt and discouragement to those seeking to do God's will.

Indeed, the Kingdom message is *the message* propelling us into the twenty-first century. New wine cannot be contained in old wineskins. No one can deny that the Spirit of the Lord is moving in this hour to cleanse the temple and purge the body of residue so that He can release His Spirit in greater measure. During this painful process, we must cooperate with the Spirit's purposes and maintain our confidence.

The media have deliberately focused upon Christianity in an attempt to destroy its credibility. Controversy, scandal and religion mixed with politics make great news stories. But God will eventually turn media attention—adverse or otherwise—into a channel to give the world His message of hope. Interspersed within the masses of those listening to Christian leaders' comments with an *inquirer's mentality* are people who are genuinely seeking answers to the complexities of life. God always answers those who seek, knock and ask.

An editorial published in the *Atlanta Journal & Constitution* written by David Edwin Harrell Jr., a University Scholar of History at the University of Alabama at Birmingham, focuses on some of the reasons that Charismatics are targets of the secular media at the moment. This article, "Watch Out for Robertson in the Southern Primaries," told as much about the secular fears of a new reformation as it did about the presidential candidacy of Pat Robertson.

"So, what can a few Pentecostals and charismatics do to the electoral process? Have you looked around at the big churches in your area lately? I don't mean those decaying mausoleums that attract a few suburban Mercedes on Sunday morning.

"I mean the Full Gospel Tabernacles in the blue-collar section and the glitzy megachurches in the suburbs. They are filled with thousands of hand-clapping, foot-stomping, heaven-bound charismatics . . . Don't underestimate these Christians. They are attractive folks. They are probably the most racially and ethnically balanced religious movement in America . . .

". . . The spread of the charismatic movement around the world is the most important Protestant story of the 20th Century and Pat Robertson is simply the American version of a worldwide revival that has changed the world's religious demography . . ."

David Edwin Harrell Jr.,
The Atlanta Journal & Constitution
"Watch Out For Robertson In The Southern Primaries,"
February 13, 1988, p. 21 A.

I agree that "the spread of the Charismatic Movement around the world is the most important Protestant story of the 20th Century . . ." Large numbers of people speak our message boldly today. Many who grew up in classical Pentecostal families as I did remember well the days of little storefront churches and the persecution of small groups of *holy rollers* in the poorer sections of town. Pentecostal women confused ugliness with holiness. Our lives were regulated by *don'ts*. Now Charismatics enjoy the trappings of social acceptability, and even spiritual acceptability until we dare to say with conviction, "Thus saith the Lord . . ." Those words trigger opposition.

We live in a time of reaping the great harvest of God. Our warfare is not against *flesh and blood*. Because the spiritual stakes are high, spirits of Accusation, Intimidation, Deception and Self-exaltation come against all Christians committed to living as witnesses in the Kingdom of God. Spiritual AIDS attacks the immunity system of the spiritual body just as AIDS debilitates the natural body. Members of the spiritual body need one another to fight off the insidious attacker. Satan knows his time is short. When Christians are fitly joined together in faith, love and purpose, powers of darkness are threatened with defeat as never before.

THE DAY OF THE LOCAL CHURCH

This is the hour for local churches to come alive. The strength and anointing of parachurch ministries will diminish unless those ministries relate their goals directly to strengthening the work of local churches. We are past the time when *lone rangers* are effective ministers. Today God is placing His blessing on ". . . the whole body, joined and knit together by what every joint supplies, according to the effective working by which every part does its share, causing growth of the body for the edifying of itself in love" (Ephesians 4:16).

God used the parachurch concept to awaken the local church into understanding that people wanted more ministry than was taking place through Sunday morning sermonettes. Plurality of ministry—blending the ministries of the apostle, prophet, evangelist, pastor and teacher—is necessary for healthy Christian growth. But a good supplementary spiritual resource becomes counterproductive and competitive if it functions as a separate entity, drawing Christians' loyalties from the vision God has given to their local assemblies.

God never intended for the parachurch to replace the function of local churches in equipping saints for the work of the ministry. Ministers who are gifts to the transcendent Church must always seek to strengthen the work of local bodies. The primary value of traveling ministries today is to knit a local church in one city to another local church thousands of miles away through spiritual cross-pollinization. I believe this singleness of direction and purpose should also be the primary goal of any outreach ministry—sounding the single blast of the trumpet of the Lord across the land, bringing God's people into singleness of heart and mind to shine as empowered witnesses for Him.

Now apostles, prophets, evangelists, pastors and

teachers ministering to the Church at large, and even traveling Christian musicians taking their ministries from city to city, will accomplish no lasting impact for God unless they honor the authority of local pastors of the cities in which they minister. These traveling ministers, themselves, must identify with a specific local church as their covering and counsel for the sake of their own spiritual well-being. They may be used in service to the transcendent Church, yet they must place themselves in genuine submission to those over them in the Lord in their own local church. Only traveling ministries with close ties to a local church will maintain effective ministry to the total body today.

So many problems in traveling ministries, including music ministries, can be avoided simply by receiving the proper covering of eldership in the body of Christ. Without spiritual counsel and covering of intercession, many traveling ministries are walking targets for Satan. These ministers need spiritual roots somewhere—an elder they can call in the middle of the night, a healthy diet of spiritual food to feed them by weekly cassette and video tapes, people who know and love them as church *members* rather than *celebrities on stage.*

ELDERS AT THE GATES

Local pastors serve as *gatekeepers* over their cities. *Gates* in Scripture represent authority. Pastors need to know one another by the Spirit and learn the strengths and needs of one another's ministries. God has assigned local pastors as *watchmen.* I meet regularly with other pastors in Atlanta—Baptists, Presbyterians, Methodists, etc., as well as other Charismatic pastors. Several of my associate pastors also serve on various ecumenical councils in Atlanta which meet to find solutions for specific problems afflicting our city. Local pastors are assigned by God to seek His will over the needs of their citizens and the direction of local city governments.

God holds local pastors accountable for the spiritual well-being of their congregations, their communities and their cities. Pastors are called to intercede and to speak out boldly on moral and civil issues. For example, we have become concerned about the safety of shoppers at the shopping mall in the neighborhood of our church. Teenagers—some with a gang mentality—have tried to take over the premises. Not only is safety an issue, the quality of merchandise is affected because shoppers are going elsewhere. We are addressing this problem in a variety of ways, including offering to help the police officers assigned to our neighborhood. We discussed the problem with them at a luncheon given in their honor sponsored by our church. We have formed our own teenaged *gang* called *Angels In Charge,* dedicated to ensuring the safety of shoppers from the stores to their cars.

A pastor must be sensitive to the needs of people living in the area where God has placed him—whether they are members of his church or not. We have begun surveying the citizens of our area with a *Real Talk Action Van,* staffed by volunteers from the church. We want to know firsthand the concerns and fears of people who live in the neighborhood of our church. We pass the surveys we take along to public officials and the press, as well as seek solutions to meet the needs of people that our ministry reaches out to help.

If the local pastor is a watchman, gatekeeper and

guardian in God's structure, doesn't it follow that Christians receiving ministry at parachurch meetings without the covering of their local pastors violate God's order and design? God will never bless those giving or receiving ministry who ignore His designated structure.

Even personal prophecies spoken over Christians at large gatherings of believers need to be submitted to those Christians' pastors in their local churches. I know of numerous examples of Christians becoming spiritually disillusioned due to unfulfilled expectations of a prophecy which they received at a large crusade, and never submitted to the elders at their own churches for spiritual discernment. Spiritual covering always brings freedom—not bondage. Christians who are reluctant to share their concerns and receive the counsel of eldership over a personal matter usually are harboring some resistance to God's will in their lives.

THE NECESSITY OF TRUST

Local churches have a great opportunity to cultivate trust in the lives of people who receive ministry. Of course, familiarity with a minister can become a barrier to faith, as with those who called Jesus "the carpenter's son." But in a day when double standards in ministry are being purged as God shakes His Church, familiarity ensures a minister's daily accountability and provides close personal care for people. Knowing one's pastor can also be a tremendous asset in the continuity of Christian growth. Christians are becoming increasingly discriminating in seeking God through the ministry of those whose lives they personally know and trust.

This point seems obvious, but I'm amazed how

often I answer questions for pastors who feel guilty concerning this problem: a person receiving ministry must perceive his own minister to be an authority called and empowered by God with an ability to hear from God. Trust always involves making a choice. A pastor cannot minister to anyone unless that person is willing to receive ministry from him.

Ministry that is not received merely becomes "pearls before swine" (Matthew 7:6). The Holy Spirit gently entreats—He never threatens or pushes one to receive truth. Jesus knocks at the door and gives each individual the right to open the door or to ignore Him. If God does not violate a person's will, neither should the local pastor. I know the painful experience of watching someone *jump off a cliff* because he refuses help. But even Jesus could do no miracles in Nazareth because the people in His hometown lacked faith in *the carpenter's son* (Mark 6:3).

Parents who criticize the preacher in front of their children have probably destroyed the ministry of that spiritual leader in the minds of their children. Whenever the children become sick or are in trouble and need the pastor to pray for them, it is unlikely that they will believe God can make any difference through that preacher's prayers. Their trust has been violated—and they probably don't even remember how or when they lost respect for spiritual headship. Where do they turn for help at a time of need instead of going to their pastor? Drugs. Bad relationships. Bars. Psychiatrists. Gangs. The occult.

Some day Christians will realize that their greatest source of help in any circumstance is their local church. God's power and anointing rest upon the local church in our day. I predict that even the gifts of the Holy Spirit will be identified less with individuals in specialized ministries and more with the ministry of pastors in local churches. People will receive healing and restoration through local assemblies at the table of the Lord, through anointed preaching, through pastoral counseling, through loving relationships and the prayers of Christian friends in covenant groups—not so much at the hands of faith healers or crusade evangelists except as they minister under the covering of local churches.

GOD GIVES THE PATTERN OF STRUCTURE

The same pattern of structure for the basic unit of human relationships—the family—is the pattern for the Church family as well. God clearly designated His ideal structure for the family as a pattern for His people, His nation, His Kingdom. The father is both the natural and the spiritual head. He assumes the responsible place of authority in the family. His position enables him to protect or to abuse the family since he provides for the family's tangible needs and their need for security.

The mother is the natural and spiritual nurturer and discerner. She is responsible primarily for ensuring proper growth, health and behavior. Children are the seed of natural and spiritual unions. They must be protected from harm, instructed in discipline and brought to an understanding of their own gifts and responsibilities as they reach maturity. These roles, and an understanding of their function, are essential in proper structure in the Church.

Family structure has become so broken in society today, it is no wonder spiritual structure has become just as nebulous to Christians in God's house. Today we see young Christian novices prophesying direction in churches. Such structure in the Church parallels young children instructing their parents when to buy a house or insisting upon what they must fix for dinner. Many churches today are run by spoiled children, both those standing at the pulpit and those sitting in the pews.

When immature Christians control a ministry, people are "tossed to and fro" by every wind of doctrine (Ephesians 4:14). Abuse of spiritual gifts creates such mixture and confusion that many people reject the validity of spiritual gifts altogether. Emotions become controlling and put pressure on those responsible for the decisions in ministry. Tantrums can change the course of a ministry and bind the work of the Holy Spirit in accomplishing His purposes.

Immature leadership causes churches to split or to lose their anointing. Often the vision of a ministry is lost as well as opportunities to make any difference in a city. In their immaturity, spiritual children fight, complain and accuse others of causing their problems. Their goals are self-serving. Only the discipline of strong spiritual fathers and mothers can correct immaturity in ministry. Usually such correction must come from one or more elders called to serve the general Church.

Strong leadership among women in the ministry can be the greatest asset or the greatest detriment to the well-being of a church family. A mother sets the atmosphere of a home. As with women who override headship in the home, dominating women can ruin the flow of anointing in a church. No wonder the Bible says that men must rule their own households before they rule in God's house (1 Timothy 3:5). I could give numerous examples of both ministries that are strong because of the leadership of godly women, and ministries that have problems caused directly by controlling women who do not understand principles of spiritual headship. For that reason, I devote a chapter in this book to the vital role of women in the ministry of the contemporary Church. The next few decades will confirm the value of godly spiritual mothers who bring unruly spiritual children to understand discipline in God's house.

God will confirm His authority and anointing in a ministry through physical and emotional health among His people. A healthy church (body) is continuously growing, learning, making a significant impact upon society. A healthy church has spiritual fathers, mothers and children at every level of spiritual maturity, living and learning together. The need for mature spiritual eldership in the local church has never been greater. The time of harvest calls for seasoned laborers who know what to do. Trust is essential for Christian growth, both individually and numerically. No ministry provides the daily accountability that can foster trust in leadership—necessary soil for the harvest—like the local church.

So if the parachurch must become a support ministry to local congregations that address the needs of their community and city, what focus does ministry outreach take? Gustav Niebuhr writes in an article, "Is Television's Golden Age Over?" that the ministry of the local church is underscored as being the trend of outreach ministry of the future:

> "William Martin, a sociologist at Rice University in Houston, said the time is coming when successful religious broadcasters will be neither talk-show hosts like Pat Robertson nor crusading evangelists like Jimmy Swaggart. Instead, he said, Christian television will be dominated by sober-faced pastors who point out that

they speak from a pulpit under the watchful eyes of a congregation and board of deacons."

Gustav Niebuhr, "Is Television's Golden Age Over?"
The Atlanta Journal & Constitution
March 20, 1988, p.7C.

SECULAR OR SPIRITUAL STRATEGY

Again, trust is essential to effective ministry. Because Christian leaders realize that trust is so necessary, an alarming trend of accountability for outreach ministries has been proposed to ensure integrity in religious broadcasting. The proposed concepts sound good initially, but I'm concerned that the long-range consequences of these proposals violate foundational, biblical principles of ministry. Such proposals are based on secular methods of checks and balances rather than scriptural ones.

The idea is to establish boards for ethics and financial accountability—imitating the concept of impartial boards like those that universities and corporations have. One stipulation of the board is that the majority of the board of directors shall be people other than employees or those joined by a family relationship—in other words, disinterested parties.

Why is an impartial board regulating ethics and finances of an outreach ministry not a good idea? It violates the scriptural patterns of structure in ministry. Any vision from God to a ministry will get lost in the shuffle—just as the vision of corporations and universities are frequently lost through the influence of wealthy board members who call the shots from a distance. Broadcaster Ted Baehr writes in an article called, "Was God a Nepotist? Protecting the Electric Pulpit from Wickedness":

107

". . . Every time an institution recruited trustees who did not understand and share the biblical vision, the organization followed the trustees', not the founders', vision. The histories of universities confirms the fact that there are no disinterested trustees, only trustees who are divorced from the life, or the vision, of the organization . . .

". . . Since Christians look at the world through the Bible, rather than the Bible through the world, we find in His Word that God never commanded His people to appoint neutral boards to govern His organizations. In fact, He appointed family members to rule His chosen people . . .

". . . Adopting the unscriptural methods of the world demonstrates a lack of trust in God and His Word, which is extremely dangerous . . .

". . . Let us not fall into the doctrinal confusion of concocting human laws to prevent a spiritual problem, a heretical approach which Paul condemns in his letter to the Galatians. We must not be intimidated by the world into adopting laws which contradict the Word of God."

Ted Baehr, "Was God A Nepotist? Protecting
the Electric Pulpit From Wickedness"
Good News! April 1988

One of the greatest challenges of the next decade will be the scriptural integrity of handling church affairs. Already some Christians are looking to civil courts, the U.S. government and the secular press to straighten out our problems. Where are trustworthy elders? Where are men of prayer who are seasoned in the Word of God? Where are the apostles and prophets? Why are we convinced that court decisions are more binding than the principles of Scripture? Which has more authority in our lives: civil law or canon law? Every Christian will be tested in his allegiance to God's Word against secular strategy within the

Church before the end of this century.

CONFESS UP

I serve as a bishop to several hundred churches around the world. That office means that I am the spiritual elder and covering of the pastors of those churches. I hear the pastors' most serious problems and share their struggles. Though I am assisted in the day to day responsibilities of the office of the bishop by one of my associate pastors, Dr. Kirby Clements, I offer counsel in making final decisions concerning direction in these ministries. I call for correction in these ministries at times. I hear confessions and restore men and women to ministry when restoration and healing are needed.

Twenty-two pastors and a staff of approximately eighty employees assist me in ministry to my local congregation at Chapel Hill Harvester Church in Atlanta. Over forty years of ministerial experience has taught me some valuable principles of structure, and I've encountered and worked through almost every structural problem in ministry. The bursting of old wineskins that I see happening in the Church today makes me know that the new wineskins of this move of God could very well contain the great harvest of the final days of human history. Finally, we are learning that being *fitly joined together* is the key to becoming the empowered witness, the Church of Jesus Christ shining as a city upon a hill, becoming salt and light to our society.

One simple little principle of ministry helps clarify many of the questions that arise every day in the ministry of Christians—both for members in churches and for those in full-time ministry: *Confess up; minister down.* What does that mean? First, any confession of sin, emotional problems, work problems, relationship problems, etc., should be shared only with those who are in structural authority over the one confessing. We should only seek help from one who is more spiritually mature, seasoned and experienced in ministry than we are.

For example, a senior pastor should never share his intimate marriage problems or sexual temptations by seeking advice from a deacon. This deacon may be trustworthy, but he is in no position to offer spiritual counsel to the senior pastor—and problems will inevitably arise from misplaced confidence. Even if the deacon offers good advice, unless God is raising this deacon to a place of spiritual authority, the vulnerability from his pastor will result in either spiritual pride or insecurity in that deacon.

Misplaced confidence can be used as pressure upon the pastor in some future situations. Obligations or fear of exposure could affect future decisions that could stop the flow of God's anointing upon that ministry. Every pastor needs seasoned spiritual elders to be his counselors without fear of future reprisals. Few deacons are spiritually able to hear a pastor's confessions without it causing serious spiritual problems in their own lives. Either the deacon is hurt spiritually and feels he must do something about the pastor's problem (which has created a problem for him), or he uses the confidential information for his own self-seeking purposes.

A work problem should probably be shared first with a supervisor, then progress *up* to those in greater authority until the matter is resolved at whatever level is necessary for a resolution. Sins and spiritual problems must be discussed with one's spiritual head, then a deacon, an elder, a pastor, etc. Again, trust is essential in ministry. Discernment is the mark of spiritual maturity.

The most frequent violations of trust involve sharing problems with someone on the same spiritual level or one who is less spiritually mature than the one sharing. I have taught my congregation to ask someone who begins *confessing* to them, "Have you talked with your pastor about this?" Too many churches are continuously disrupted by busybodies who want to *fix* other people's lives.

Spiritual maturity means that a person does not want to know *everything* because he realizes the responsibility that comes with highly classified information. Not all problems even need to be shared with people closest to us in relationships. This is a valuable lesson for ministers. Even a husband or a wife does not need to know every problem at the church. How vital this lesson is in our day!

If a matter is concerning life or death, it must come to my attention as the senior pastor of our local church. I insist upon hearing the discussions surrounding a couple's decision to get a divorce, for example, because often children's lives are at stake. If both parties are Christians and respect spiritual authority, perhaps the marriage can be saved. Nevertheless, I am responsible to cover the victims of a broken home and ensure their spiritual, emotional and physical care.

I hear confessions concerning abortion because for whatever reason, that decision involved the interruption of a human life. I must be the pastor to help families decide whether or not to take a loved one off life-support mechanisms if the doctors offer no hope of recovery. Only a senior pastor can help that young woman or that family face the emotional consequences of life and death decisions and pick up the pieces of their lives after such decisions are carried out.

Every Wednesday I meet with the shepherding pastors of my Presbytery to share the serious pastoral concerns of ministry at Chapel Hill Harvester Church. The secretaries are dismissed, and in a closed session we discuss the best direction over specific problem areas in people's lives. We take seriously the charge to watch over those entrusted by God to our care. Keeping a confidence is one of the most vital requirements for a pastor. Our callings are confirmed by our ability to hear from God over the lives of His lambs and bring healing, restoration and health to shattered lives by following God's direction. If we don't know the answers, it's our responsibility to pray until God gives direction to us or performs a miracle. He is the great Counselor!

MINISTER DOWN

So what does *minister down* mean? A person should never try to minister beyond his level of spiritual confidence and personal experience. One element of spiritual maturity which is not emphasized enough is knowing one's limitations in ministry. We are fitly joined together to cover one another's weaknesses and draw upon one another's strengths.

An older Christian wife and mother may be the best minister to train young wives how to love their husbands and care for their young children. That same woman is not necessarily spiritually equipped to pray for someone to receive the baptism in the Holy Spirit or to help a couple make the decision to have another baby. Christian teenagers make excellent ministers to younger children in areas of behavioral discipline and family and social relationships, but they are not necessarily good Bible teachers to children.

Men and women called by God to serve as apostles, prophets, evangelists, pastors and teachers should also stay within their callings unless and until God changes the dimensions of their ministries. If that change occurs, the ones over them in the Lord are in agreement to confirm new direction. Consistently bearing good spiritual fruit becomes the sign of God's confirmation in ministry because God uses fruit to identify the trees. Good spiritual fruit always brings honor and glory to God and increases the influence of His Kingdom. It never draws attention and glory to the tree except as a source of satisfying food from God.

The contemporary Church is hindered in its mission by ministers trying to fulfill someone else's calling. Too often, music ministers want to prophesy. Pastors try to establish new churches. Apostles want to stay at home and counsel people. Intercessors want to preach. Our callings from God always mean self-denial and taking up a cross daily. Somewhere ministers have gotten the idea that ministry must gratify the flesh with a continuous mountaintop experience—or it isn't from God. This problem is so widespread that it is certainly a tactic of the enemy to keep the bones of the body of Christ disjointed and unable to function properly.

When people minister within their callings, the entire body of Christ is edified and strengthened. No wonder the warfare is so great over callings! Pride, ambition, jealousy, criticism and lack of cooperation cripple the ministry of the local church. No one wins. When one minister fails, we all fail; when one minister flows in anointing in his calling, we all benefit.

And remember, sometimes God chooses the ones who are not as attractive, talented or obviously equipped for an assignment as the ones we would choose. He still chooses *foolish things* to show forth His glory! God delights in showing forth His strength through human weaknesses. As a senior pastor, I continually ask God for spiritual vision in identifying the ministers He chooses.

SUBMISSION TO HEADSHIP

I think that it is important to state emphatically that no minister is beyond the need for covering, counsel and spiritual headship. I am a bishop, and I eagerly submit to those whom God has given to me as elders over my ministry and my personal life. Several times I have laid the future of Chapel Hill Harvester Church at an elder's feet and vowed to abide by his counsel on serious matters of closing our doors or pressing forward. I could name the names of men of God to whom I am submitted without a moment's hesitation. They know well the responsible role God has given to them in guiding my decisions. I want correction and advice! I do not trust any minister who refuses to seek the counsel of eldership!

So what of the warnings and lessons of the Shepherding Movement? Isn't teaching on submission to spiritual headship dangerous? Should we not be afraid of extremes? I say let's learn lessons from the mistakes of the Shepherding Movement and not repeat them. The Holy Spirit is never a taskmaster bringing people into bondage. Godly counsel never violates God's Word, God's character nor a Christian's conscience when it is controlled by the Holy Spirit, and Jesus is the Lord of that Christian's life.

But please hear me: we should not throw out the

baby with the bath water! Mistakes, errors, abuses and misinterpretations never change truth from the Lord! The Church will never, never come to a maturity of faith without an understanding of callings, headship and submission to the authority God has placed in His body. Without definable headship, we can never become the army of the Lord with the overcoming power to defeat the enemy. Instead, the Church is fragmented, disjointed and every man is a god unto himself.

The coming together of elders at the same level of ministry is extremely important to be fitly joined together in the fivefold ministry of the Church at large. Examples of these meetings would be the interdenominational meetings of pastors in Atlanta as I have mentioned, or Charismatic Bible Ministries, or the Network of Christian Ministries, or the Idea Exchange of pastors with churches having one thousand or more members, or Robert Schuller's super-church pastors' retreat with their wives in an informal setting. If a minister has not had the privilege of serving several thousand members, he cannot give advice on managing a ministry of that scope to a pastor who has. Some lessons of maturity—both failures and successes—come only with experience.

PASSING THE BATON

Experience is also a central issue in *passing the baton* of ministry from one generation to another. I am alarmed at the ambition I detect in many young ministers today. They believe that the old guard needs to get out of their way and let them take the wheel. Such attitudes will wreck the ship on the rocks as well as the lives of these young ministers. They do not understand even the basic lessons of Scripture concerning calling, anointing and timing under the Holy Spirit's direction.

God only raises up leaders when He chooses—otherwise, they may spend years in the pasture caring for sheep, or hiding in caves from their enemies, or sitting in prison until Pharaoh calls them to be a solution to their generation. Leadership does not begin when one is ordained as a bishop or stands behind a pulpit. God chooses leaders to plan major conferences who begin by planning picnics. A youth pastor may be at the peak of his ministry when he makes a difference in the life and death decision of a teen contemplating suicide or having an abortion. Who measures greatness in ministry? What is the criteria? Numbers of members? No! Extent of one's influence? No! A great spiritual leader is one who is obedient to God's will in his own life and in the lives of those whom God has entrusted to his care.

The greater the responsibility in ministry, the greater the price that comes with it, and the more stringent the training period. The proving ground for leaders is often illogical—a good woman pastor may spend her youth changing diapers and mopping floors faithfully. An apostle may spend years keeping the grounds of the church, planting flowers, cutting grass and trimming shrubbery. Men look at the outward signs of leadership—intelligence, aggressiveness, talent, personal charisma and physical attractiveness—but God looks at the heart. When God decides the time has come to pass the baton, no one needs to wrestle it away from another.

I ran track in college. One interesting detail of winning a relay race was passing the baton. The one receiving the baton runs alongside the one who is passing it. For several yards, the two runners run in stride together. What a spiritual example of passing responsibility from one generation to another.

The future leaders of the Church must run in stride with the generals in God's army today. They must feel the pace that is already set. They must assume the same pressure, responsibility and goal of winning the race, years before they run alone. I appreciate so much the spirit and mature wisdom of one of my spiritual sons, Dennis Peacocke, who said recently, "When I am sitting in a meeting discussing matters of direction for the Church, I like to see a lot of gray-haired men around the table." Such an attitude indicates the qualities of a true leader, designated for greater responsibility in the days ahead. The greatest teachers always begin as dedicated students, absorbing every detail of their lessons until God decides it is graduation day.

HIS DWELLING PLACE

New wineskins! New structure to contain the spiritual life of the time of harvest. What a day God has allowed us to experience! I've come to a new understanding of *the place* Jesus said that He was going to prepare for us (John 14:2). I believe that Jesus prepares a *dwelling place* for us through the continual intercession He makes in our behalf. This dwelling place is the presence of God. This dwelling place is proper positioning in the body of Christ—not so much a *mansion in the sky in the sweet by and by* as we have thought, but instead a dwelling place in God's presence today as we are fitly joined together as the body of Christ.

Properly positioned, we are able to see the Father (John 14:3-9). In that dwelling place we come into intimate relationship with God the Father through

117

Jesus Christ our Lord. Corporately, we become the very dwelling place of God. The Church is instructed to "forsake not the assembling of yourselves together" (Hebrews 10:25), and "where two or three are gathered together in My name, I am there in the midst of them" (Matthew 18:20). He dwells in the praises of His people (Psalm 22:3). This dwelling place is a place of covenant—under His wings, in the shadow of the Almighty (Psalm 91).

Do we realize how desperately our world needs to see God? They will see Him clearly as the Church becomes more aware of the reality of new wineskins, His dwelling place. Jesus asked His disciples,

Do you not believe that I am in the Father, and the Father in Me? The words that I speak to you I do not speak on My own authority; but the Father who dwells in Me does the works. Believe Me that I am in the Father and the Father in Me, or else believe Me for the sake of the works themselves. (John 14:10,11)

Is the Church able to say those words to the world? Can they see our good works and glorify the Father Who is in heaven? Hardly! They see our fighting, our scandals, our competition and our worldly goals. Do we even understand what *works* will show them the Father? What were the works of Jesus?

Jesus declares that He came to destroy the works of the devil (1 John 3:8). That is also our calling—to destroy deception, oppressive governments, oppressive religions, anything that limits the quality of life that God wants man to enjoy. Jesus opened blinded eyes, deaf ears, healed the lame, opened the prison of circumstances to set the captives free. We must also do those works—so that the world can see the Father.

118

And whatever you ask in My name, that I will do, that the Father may be glorified in the Son. If you ask anything in My name, I will do it. (John 14:13,14)

Could God trust the Church with anything she asked? I believe that God is bringing the Church into a position in which we will know the reality of this promise. This promise can only be granted to one who is beloved like the Shulamite maiden in Song of Solomon, or Esther as she stood before the king. This promise is made to a mature woman who is ready for marriage. Such a promise would destroy an immature little girl.

In proper position in God, we will only ask those things which are in God's character and in accordance with His will. Our requests will never violate His holiness. We will not ask selfishly to our own advantage, but to His advantage. In His dwelling place we are so absolutely integrated into God's Spirit that we could not possibly think or ask anything apart from His plan and His will.

New wine in new wineskins! God is building a dwelling place for Himself among people with open hearts, anointed ears and boldness in their mouths. They are willing and ready to do the works of Jesus to show forth the Father to a world desperately needing to see Him. Out of new wineskins, life will pour forth—abundant, righteous, peaceful, healing, passionate, challenging, exciting, joyful, productive, creative, wholesome and fresh! And the world will come to quench their thirsty minds, heal their broken hearts and feed their hungry souls.

Chapter Five
Spiritual Trends

† The role of women will continue to be a primary target of spiritual warfare.

† Instability in the identity of women will become more obvious as the reason for instability of the home and the Church—as will the host of social problems related to that instability.

† As women resolve their identity crises, the Church will begin to mature rapidly.

† The emerging extremes in the media of *little girl* and *seductress* as examples of *spiritual women* will continue to place the proper role of Christian women in a precarious position.

† Women will seek proper headship as they realize the difference between freedom under male covering and suppression under male rule.

† Women will begin to challenge the deception of social pressures robbing them of their self-esteem in the priority of their calling to minister to the family.

† *Women only* or *men only* ministries will die spiritually because they are a detriment to Kingdom purposes and because they impair the ability to minister in balance according to God's plan.

† Kingdom women will undeniably be the most attractive women in the world, setting standards in fashion and beauty.

† The ministry of effective intercession will flourish among women in the Church because they are gifted as natural mediators and will be used at a time when intercession is most vital to fulfilling the mission of the Church.

† The Church will recognize the gift of feminine discernment as essential for proper growth and strategy in all aspects of ministry.
† Women will begin to see their husbands, children, and others by their spiritual identities instead of by their natural identities.
† Christian women will set the standards for freedom, security, confidence and authority for women around the world.

5

SPIRITUAL EQUAL RIGHTS

Who is she? Little girl? Seductress? Shrewd woman on the board of directors? Pastor in the pulpit? Glorified maid, chauffeur and cook? Understandably, the role of women in modern society is at the root of some of the most highly contested issues for debate. The gender gap. Abortion. Daycare. Consumer goods. Equal job opportunities. Divorce, alimony and child custody. Tax reform. Prostitution. Pornography. Women have wrestled with the question of their identity for centuries. Why are women's issues still so volatile as we approach the twenty-first century? In spite of shifting values in society causing varying definitions of the family, the wife/mother is the central role in determining the atmosphere—therefore, the stability—of the home. Likewise, women in ministry are essential to fulfilling the commission of the Church family. *She* remains a primary target of spiritual warfare.

We need only review the lessons of history to recognize the significance of women causing men, empires, nations and civilizations to rise to victory or to crumble in defeat. When *she* becomes a force of evil, few are strong enough to stand against her powers of manipulation. Of course the same is true whenever *she* decides to fight for good causes by utilizing her unsurpassed powers to persuade others.

Recent scandals in major ministries involving sexual sins have placed the role of women in the Church in a freshly precarious place. Sadly, extremes are again determining the place of Christian women in ministry. Many of the most visible women in Christian television, for example, have prompted some Christian women to accept the *little girl* image as a standard for spirituality.

Little girls are perceived as being safe and nonthreatening. These women deliberately suppress their intelligence. They giggle and cry easily. Though they are cute, entertaining and frivolous in a way which is endearing, they lack spiritual depth in discussing solutions to major problems confronting our world. Perhaps more than they know, they represent the bride of Christ who is in reality a *little girl,* still unprepared to be a comparable helpmeet to Christ. *Little girls* will never make a difference in the world for the gospel of the Kingdom.

The other extreme is the seductive woman who sets out to use her sexual attractiveness to control or to destroy. She is calculating and dangerous. This extreme is the historical basis for the Fundamentalists' insistence on women wearing long dresses, no make-up or jewelry and hair pulled back into a ball on top of their heads, etc. Because feminine beauty can possibly become destructive to spirituality, extremists overreacted, preaching plainness as a desirable spiritual standard for women.

No one denies that seductive women are controlled by forces of darkness and find gratification in causing men and ministries to fall. However, I am appalled that Christian women feel guilty for the natural beauty God has given them because ungodly women misuse theirs. They are being tricked into inhibition in worship for fear they will attract (or distract) someone standing near them from focusing on God. They are being accused of wrong motives for faithfulness in participating in church activities, giving financial contributions to the church, ministering to men of God in some helpful, personal way, or having close friendships with Christian men other than their husbands. Accusations of seduction prevent them from being bold witnesses for the sake of the gospel. And I say that Satan is their accuser. Committed Christian women are a major threat to the powers of darkness.

What are the innate qualities women bring to the ministry that ignite such warfare over their identities? Women are natural discerners over the lives of those whom they love. They know instinctively how to correct and to protect people at the same time. Women are masters at public relations and evangelism. Their confidence in their husbands is an unparalleled factor in giving men the fortitude to act responsibly. They know how to restore wounded people. Women are primarily the nurturers of the seed of covenant from one generation to another.

No wonder the battle rages over the role of women. That role has taken on such extremes in an attempt to thwart women's rightful place in ministry. If Satan cannot intimidate her and lock her away, he will attempt to make her into an ineffective or dangerous distortion of God's perfect plan for her life and her mission in His Church.

THE WARFARE OVER WOMEN

The source of spiritual warfare over the role of women began in the garden when God pronounced the curses for Eve's deception and Adam's sin (Genesis 3). Because of disobedience and deception, God appointed man to rule over woman. He set enmity between the seed of the woman and the serpent—an enmity which has served to press women in a subservient caste throughout generations and even continues to press them in many cultures today. Forces of darkness hate women who fulfill their callings from God because they break the power of the curse through covenant in Jesus Christ. Through Jesus Christ's atonement, women are set free from the bondage of suppression to enjoy the freedom of spiritual covering. There is neither male nor female in Jesus Christ (Galatians 3:28). No women on earth are more free to be who God created them to be than Spirit-filled women who know their identities in Christ.

To most feminists, headship is a dirty word. We must never underestimate the influence of feminism in our culture. Family concerns rank as a low priority to many young women today. Our lifestyles have programmed us to desire instant rewards and immediate returns on our investments. The rapid feedback of moving ahead in a professional career challenges the long-range, intrinsic values of the full-time wife-mother-nurturer.

Becoming a homemaker is no longer considered to be a respectable goal for young women in a society that honors intellect and marketable skills. Motherhood has been reduced to a brief interruption in the pursuit of career goals. The demands of contemporary living push women into the labor force in order to maintain intellectual respect as well as to ensure the high standards of living that most families demand.

The media convince women that they can *have it all*. They are increasingly persuaded that their value and self-esteem in life is more often found in productive careers than in limiting themselves to the *meager rewards* that come with nurturing their children. Though so many symptomatic problems of unstable family life plague our society—drugs, crime, suicide, illiteracy, etc.—women have bought the myth that their investments in family life are not as important as meaningful careers are in contributing to a high standard of living and to cultural advancement.

Allow me to state emphatically that I am not opposed to working wives and mothers. I understand that many women must work outside their homes to offer their families necessities and even additional, tangible benefits provided from their salaries. We employ many mothers on our staff at Chapel Hill Harvester Church who are also excellent homemakers. My emphasis focuses upon examining the dangerous social pressures influencing women. I take issue with current social priorities and values that destroy the family. We are caught in a social trajectory threatening family stability, and the role of women is the major contingent in this breakdown. Disintegrating family values are the root of many other important issues.

Let me add that I am convinced some women are better wives and mothers because they work outside the home. I find no virtue in the stereotyped housewife who spends hours talking on the telephone, gossiping with the neighbors or watching television soap operas. In spite of maintaining a demanding pace, many Christian wives and mothers work in professions and still maximize family time by giving careful attention toward developing harmonious family relationships.

At the same time, I object to degrading the role of a *homemaker* as a less valuable contribution to our society than women working in business or medical careers, for example. The homemaker's contribution to society is probably greater, or at least as great, as that of women working in socially significant careers. Pressures to pursue careers manipulate women. Social conformity almost always impedes the will of God in the lives of Christian women.

The impartation of a godly mother's spirit to her children cannot be duplicated by others. Timing is extremely important to decisions related to bringing up children. Church leaders must be sensitive to God's direction to individual women in their specific circumstances. Some women need to earn incomes for the best interests of their families. Other women need the discipline to manage financially on their husbands' salaries and devote their full time to raising children.

Perhaps God calls some women to set aside professional skills for a season during the formative years in their children's lives when parental role models serve as a major influence. Other women are given God's direction to handle multi-faceted responsibilities with grace. To insist that some women remain at home would be as abusive as insisting that some wives and mothers work outside their homes to find fulfillment. The focus should be on maintaining the priorities of a wife and mother according to the standards of abundant life recorded in God's Word.

A Christian woman must seek first the Kingdom of God to discover her own particular place in ministry. She must be willing to give her individual talents to serve God in the Church in our generation. I believe that the acceleration of the tug-of-war women experience today has deliberately coincided with the opening of the greatest doors of opportunity that Christian women have ever known. Worldly doors are also opening. Instead of viewing her career as a calling and seizing her opportunities to advance the message of the Kingdom, worldly rewards entice women to be commercially competitive to gain higher paying positions and greater socio-economic status.

Indisputably, women play an essential role in the great harvest of these last days. God consistently uses women to ensure the implementation of His will. God has gifted women with invaluable abilities to comprehend spiritual direction. Women must become involved in carrying out God's plan. The ingathering of the great harvest of *spiritual babies* calls for mature Kingdom *mothers* to feed, protect and discipline those babes in Christ as they grow. Christian women should set the standards for beauty, fashion and talent and provide solutions to problems.

The Bible says much about the role of women and their powerful influence upon both worldly kingdoms and the Kingdom of God. Though legalistic Church traditions have sometimes been suppressive toward women, Christianity has liberated women in every culture around the world where the gospel has been received. I agree with Bible teachers who interpret Paul's warning about women not speaking in Church as being a way of protecting the early Church from persecution (1 Corinthians 14:34). Since Jewish women were to remain silent, any place of worship where women were speaking in freedom indicated that these were Christians gathered—making them an easy prey for persecution. One of the greatest threats to the survival of the early Church was the freedom of women!

God has trusted women with some of His most important assignments. Remember, God and one woman brought redemption to the earth. Mary's answer to the angel who brought her a disturbing announcement is a resounding weapon in the lives of women of harvest today. Mary responded, ". . . Let it be done to me according to your word" (Luke 1:38). Such yielding to the plan of God among spiritual women will birth the great harvest in our generation. The eyes of God search the earth for modern *Marys* whom He can trust to yield to His plan and to follow His direction without wavering because of the personal price in carrying out His word.

Many times God's direction seems puzzling or disturbing. Why? God's direction leads us into direct confrontation with worldly spirits of atheism, lawlessness and mammon in order to demonstrate His alternative to worldly thinking and behavior. There are wilderness experiences and desert places in following God's will. Mary's declaration of total surrender to God's will becomes an example of Kingdom faith. Any situation becomes triumphant when we trust God's view of the *big picture* before we are able to see the end of the path clearly for ourselves. The

Kingdom of God is built in trust. We must learn to trust God, and even more difficult, to trust *the Christ* in one another. Spiritual confirmation by God-appointed headship in the Church is essential to women finding direction from the Lord for their lives. Too many women are disregarding headship and declaring themselves as their own authorities.

I am alarmed at the presumption I discern in many women's ministries today. Several years ago, God showed me that a Vashti spirit had infiltrated the Church through women who separated themselves from the total direction of God's plan in this critical hour. Many of these women's ministries have insisted upon doing their *own thing,* activities which may seem to be wholesome on the surface, but actually promote God's cause very little and become counter-productive to women joining them who are sincerely seeking God's plan for their lives. These ministries plan *banquets for the women, then refuse to subject themselves to the bidding of the King (Esther 1:9-22).*

After I taught this insight, I received some unfavorable letters from women accusing me of having a *chauvinistic* view of ministry. Nothing could be further from the truth! The blending of men and women on my Presbytery and staff should lay to rest any accusations that I close the doors of ministry at the most responsible levels of leadership to anyone whom God ordains. My calling from the Lord is to confront any type of prejudice in God's Church. I have been given a message of spiritual equal rights to proclaim to the body of Christ.

I do detect tremendous danger in women moving outside of their purposes in God's creation of them as women—body, soul and spirit. Like it or not, God created woman because man was lonely and needed a helper. God created woman to complete man. Though God is complete within Himself and never experienced the fellowship of an equal companion, He recognized man's innate loneliness and need for completion in another being.

FITLY JOINED TOGETHER

I will be bold and accept the challenges of those who disagree with me. I realize that many will react to this statement: God made man and woman incomplete without each other. God insists upon harmony and completion in His creation in order to bless it. Sopranos and altos lack a full chord without the tenors and basses blending with them to give a rich, full sound. Nature consistently enforces this law in the higher forms of life. Male and female are joined to bring life and productivity to creation at every level—to replenish the chaotic conditions on earth with Kingdom order and design.

Even unmarried members of the Church must be *fitly joined together* by the Holy Spirit to other members in the Church for the work of the ministry. Platonic relationships in God's will are especially important to unmarried Christians. Pastors must be sensitive to the needs of Christian singles and provide covering in proper relationships where singles are fulfilled without temptations or threats.

Covenant communities can fill the void of a companion in a single Christian's life. However, isolation is sometimes the result of selfishness. Those who isolate themselves from spiritual fellowship will never be able to bear spiritual fruit. God designed His creation so that without the harmonious interaction of male and female on every level—body, soul and spirit—life on our planet will not survive.

Spiritual order follows God's laws of natural order. Men and women cannot bear natural children separated from one another. So it is with spiritual children born into the Kingdom of God. I cannot emphasize enough how important this understanding becomes to women of the harvest in fulfilling their mission in these last days. Satan will use every diversion possible to hinder implementation of God's will. Women in ministry who do not receive covering and counsel from men quickly get out of balance and fall into error. Men in ministry who do not open themselves to women's discernment, intercession and comfort on their behalf will either be destroyed by the enemy or will never be effective for the Lord.

Neither male nor female will survive without the other in the onslaught of the mighty spiritual battles before the coming of Christ. God has ordained interdependency within His body. Men and women must recognize that their inseparability is necessary to bear spiritual fruit which shall remain throughout eternity. No one reaches his own potential in the work of the Lord without joining in spiritual unity with other members of the body of Christ.

THE KINGDOM WOMEN

So how do Christian women avoid the extremes of becoming the *little girl* or the *seductress*? How do they relate properly to men in the work of the ministry? How do they minister in maximum spiritual strength and yet remain free under the covering of spiritual headship? Do they pursue careers or not? Women of the harvest reach their full spiritual potential aiding others in ministry. This is the secret to spiritual equal rights and to serving in the Kingdom of God as mighty spiritual women.

Aid is another word for helping and comforting. Any woman who reacts to the role of aiding someone as demeaning is already unfit for Kingdom service. Her motivations are self-serving. Examine God's purposes at creation. Review the attitudes of godly women throughout the Scriptures. Note the patterns in the lives of women in God's Word whom He raised up as spiritual examples to women today.

Yes, the same characteristics biblical, godly women exemplified will bring victory in our society, even with its unbiblical values. True, the qualities of women of harvest will be confronted, but they will also win the battles against oppressive forces. People committed to God's will cannot lose. Let's examine the characteristics of godly women throughout the Word of the Lord using the letters which spell *Aid*.

The first letter in the word *Aid* is *A* which stands for *attractiveness*. God's Word consistently proves that godly women are attractive. As I stated previously, in my Pentecostal background we were totally misled into believing that *ugly* meant *holy*. Thank God, He pushed past those pharisaical concepts to bring us into a true understanding of spiritual righteousness and the *beauty* of holiness. We know from Scripture that Sarah, Rebekah, Rachel, Esther, Ruth and other women whom God used in His covenant plan were beautiful women. Their beauty was actually a factor used in accomplishing God's will.

A woman's effectiveness in ministry depends upon her self-image according to God's master plan. Self-image and self-confidence are synonymous. Women who perceive themselves to be unattractive, unworthy and insufficient cannot possibly aid anyone in fulfilling Kingdom purposes that God has ordained. Let me state emphatically that attractiveness is not the result of wearing expensive clothes and applying make-up to perfection. Attractiveness does not necessarily depend on physical attributes.

Applying make-up represents an inward need God put within women to express and to enhance their beauty. Some women make a horrible mess of that expression! Remember that God did not place a *beauty shop* within the Garden. I'm certainly not criticizing that source of help. Some women need all the help they can find! The point I want to underscore is that *beauty* is an inward quality. No matter how much effort is given to improving the outward appearance, God does not notice. God searches the heart, not the outward appearance (1 Samuel 16:7).

Most women array themselves to impress other women. They compare themselves among themselves while the fashion industry gets rich. Few men are impressed by women wearing the latest fashions. In fact, men back away from women who are stiff and perfectly coiffured. A woman who is stiff does not meet the needs of a man. Her make-up is easily smeared, and then he feels as if he has interfered with her efforts to maintain her *image*. She has dressed to satisfy her comparison of herself with other women. Her concern has obviously not been to please the man in her life.

Modern fashions would be quite different if women were dressing to please God, or even to please men. Many fashion designers are men controlled by effeminate spirits. Modern fashions hide the natural attributes of femininity, thereby failing to accentuate the attractiveness of a woman. Yet even spiritual women allow current fashions to dictate their appearances and concepts of attractiveness.

I know that to some Christians current fashions

may seem to be a minor point, but I recognize fashion trends as one grip of Satan in many women's lives. Women of harvest must pull down this stronghold and become examples to the world in this area. Otherwise, our witness remains incomplete.

We cannot allow the standards for feminine beauty to be under the control of this world. The attractiveness of spiritual women, according to God's standards, is essential to the witness of the Church. As long as cover girls on secular magazines set standards of beauty for Christian women, the attractiveness which God has given to women is controlled by Satan's dictates in his domain. I am expecting major breakthroughs from Christian women in setting standards in beauty and the fashion arts to express that beauty.

Attractiveness is never derived by things that can be put on or taken off. Beauty is an inward quality, an inner essence. Beauty flows from one in whom the heart of a husband can safely trust. Beauty flows from one who understands the ways of the Lord. Godly wisdom makes a woman beautiful. Even before the king chose Esther as his queen, she had to be attractive to herself.

Anything superficial, make-up or clothes that could be taken away from Esther, did not make her attractive. Any beauty that can be dismantled by man is not the beauty given by God. The source of godly beauty is within the heart and can never be splattered on the outside. The source of true beauty is the spirit; the quiet considerations of life.

Esther pleased the guardians God had placed as headship over her life. First Esther pleased Mordecai, her uncle, a type of the Holy Spirit. She followed his advice implicitly (Esther 2:10, 20). Secondly, she pleased Hegai, a eunuch in charge of the women (Esther 2:8,9). Regard for the headship God had placed in her life made Esther a woman who was pleased with herself (Esther 2:15). She had total confidence that she was in God's will. She stood before the king as a woman who knew who she was—and therefore, she pleased him (Esther 2:17).

Women of the harvest must know who they are. Until they do, instead of aiding others, they are a burden. Instead of headship guiding them in positive ways which benefit the Kingdom, they must always defend and protect them as they would a little child. The *little girl* extreme can easily hide behind a cloak which appears to be submission to headship, but the results are unhealthy and unproductive. She is usually an emotional drain on the one who attempts to cover her. She is never able to stand alone for anything.

In such unhealthy relationships, headship must always act in the role of defender. The root of such relationships is usually a woman who feels incomplete and inadequate. Any man who allows a woman to remain as a child is doing her no favor. Both are incomplete in that relationship. Instead of growing to maturity, she constantly needs someone to defend her in order to reinforce her sense of security. He finds security in the relationship in the fact that he is so needed by her, so he constantly makes himself her knight in shining armor, rushing to her rescue. Proper regard for headship gave Esther the confidence in herself to stand alone before the king.

Women of the harvest must come to spiritual attractiveness by the power of the Holy Spirit. Outward expressions of beauty reveal the inner condition of the heart. When the wrinkles increase and the body does not appear as firm as it once did without effort, a woman is still beautiful because she draws the essence of beauty from the proper source that is timeless. To be the helpmeet, support and comfort that God has called women of the harvest to be, they must radiate the fresh attractiveness of the Holy Spirit.

The second quality of aiding others is the letter *I* which represents *Intercession.* Women are innately designed by God as intercessors. Spiritual sensitivity and the powers of influence are gifts from the Lord which are primarily feminine attributes. These attributes can also become extremely dangerous when the powers of darkness control them. A danger to an intercessor is developing the attitude that *God listens to me* instead of *I listen to Him.* A self-serving attitude always destroys the power of intercession and the enemy uses this tactic to hinder the flow of God's intervention in behalf of His Church.

Intercession must become a constant state of being for women of harvest—not merely a habitual part of worship. Why did Satan approach Eve instead of Adam? The serpent cut off Adam's intercessor and implementor. The serpent knew that he would destroy both of them through the error of Eve's reasoning—following the dictates of her mind instead of following spiritual direction.

The Scripture speaks of a woman's hair representing the *glory of God* (1 Corinthians 11:15). No wonder women generally give such attention to their hair—perhaps not even realizing the spiritual significance of that feature. The Apostle Paul said that it is shameful for a man to give the same degree of attention to his hair as a woman does (1 Corinthians 11:14). The emphasis is not on hair, but on the symbol of God's glory, and the representation of headship and submission in regard to a woman's role in intercession.

Anna stands as an excellent example of an intercessor. She had been married for seven years, perhaps meaning a complete relationship since seven represents the number of completion throughout Scripture. After her husband's death, the Scripture indicates that she lived eighty-four years as a widow, interceding daily in the house of God. She is the woman who prophesied over Jesus to His mother in the temple.

Intercessors always recognize Jesus by the power of the Holy Spirit. They see Him in others, never looking at mankind's flesh with judgment or condemnation. They look upon people and circumstances with spiritual vision and feel the perceptions of God's heart. Judgment and intercession are totally incompatible and contradictory. True intercessors are people who are filled with compassion. Those who are judgmental and who choose to sit in *Moses' seat* always lose any ability to intercede for others.

For eighty-four years Anna represented man to God. While the role of a prophet is representing God to man, the intercessor represents man to God. That focus of communion between God and man, joined together in ministry, is essential. Any prophetic voice must have committed intercessors to fulfill the prophetic ministry. One without the other is incomplete in revelation and demonstration of God's Word.

As intercessors, women of the harvest become *aides* in every aspect of restoration in the Kingdom of God. Intercession means *standing between*. Women are experts at standing in the gap, serving as either peacemakers or troublemakers. Few men are naturally peacemakers, but most women are born with that ability. Unfortunately, men get themselves upon the *couches of life* and don't know how to get up again. Women have the ability to change their perspectives—to *reverse* their negative perceptions into positive ones. The intercession of a godly woman can *fix* any situation by her praying to God Who changes her attitude and the attitudes of those around her.

The third letter in the word *aid* is *D* which stands for the quality of discernment. God can never trust women with the responsibility of attractiveness and the power of intercession unless they also have discernment. Spiritual discernment prevents attractiveness from becoming self-serving and vain. Lucifer allowed his beauty to make him vain, destructive and rebellious against God Who created him. I have taught that discernment is the mark of a spiritually mature Church. Likewise, discernment is the mark of a spiritually mature woman. Lack of discernment is described, "As a ring of gold in a swine's snout, so is a lovely woman who lacks discretion" (Proverbs 11:22). Lack of discernment is compared to dressing up a pig with gold jewelry.

The book of Proverbs also gives an excellent description of a discerning woman. The virtuous woman attends to the needs of her husband and her household (Proverbs 31). Her lamp does not go out at night because she discerns in the darkness, problems that could arise (verse 18). She sees to proper clothing (or covering) for her household (verse 21).

Women of the harvest must carefully discern the needs and spiritual growth of their children. Intercession alone will never replace responsible discernment over one's own household. Children are fruit, the primary responsibility of a woman's discernment.

To ignore one's discernment causes God to withhold His trust.

The Bible says that a child who gets his own way brings shame to his mother, not his father (Proverbs 29:15). I am alarmed at the attitude of women who insist that child care be divided equally with their husbands. I don't hold to that philosophy at all. No one is as responsible for the care of children as their mothers. Without exception, children are a mother's first responsibility. A mother will give an account to God in eternity for the care and nurture of the children entrusted to her.

If I were to choose from many women in the Bible who represent discernment, I would choose a young teenage girl who was still under the influence of her parents. In fact, they had arranged her betrothal to Joseph. Our culture has so distorted God's plan in relationships that we seldom realize that such weighty matters are family decisions. Again, the discernment of parents is vital to the well-being of their children.

I have three daughters. My oldest daughter, Becky, married Sam, a strong spiritual man who is one of the most discerning and prophetic pastors called to our ministry in Atlanta. Now, Becky was a very unusual teenager in that she never dated very much nor wanted to date. Whenever I would talk to her about her social life, she would simply smile and say, "Daddy, the Lord has the right man for me!"

Sam, a Californian who taught school and coached football, visited my older sister and her husband who introduced him to our family. Becky never said a word to anyone about her impression of Sam. In a few days Sam came to me—notice, he came to Becky's father—and said that he believed that Becky

141

was the woman who would become his wife. He had even received prophecy and had seen spiritual visions of her before they met.

Did I object to his pursuing my daughter? When I asked Becky concerning her feelings for Sam, she burst out crying. I knew she had fallen madly in love. I began to make arrangements for them to be together more to know the mind of the Lord, and in a few months they were married. Some would say that this story is an exception, but it certainly should not be! God gives discernment to families and will confirm His plan in their lives.

This teenage girl, Mary, had a visit from an angel who told her that she would have a baby. In spite of the gossip and disgrace this divine proclamation meant to Mary in her everyday circumstances, she responded in perfect faith to God's will. The Scriptures give no indication that Mary ever wavered in faith. We are told a very key phrase that gives insight into Mary's character, "She pondered it [God's will and His Word] in her heart."

Women without the discipline to ponder the mysteries of God within their hearts lose God's trust in showing them His truth. Too many women can't wait to tell everything they know. Every secret insight that God gives privately is lost whenever they tell it. Telling promises that God has spoken to one's heart in quiet meditation and intimacy of communion with God is error. The promise is lost because it is no longer a hidden treasure.

Only once did Mary use her natural relationship to pressure Jesus into moving in a spiritual matter (John 2:1-5). From the response that Jesus gave His mother, we know that Mary was in error. The fact that Mary brought the problem of *no wine* to Jesus indicated that she knew His power. But to take the initiative to pressure Jesus into ministry was a controlling gesture. Women who fail in discerning the spirits of their husbands or situations where God can use them lose their spiritual harmony with God's will.

How did Jesus answer her? "Woman . . ." Notice He did not call her *Mother*. That gentle rebuke closed Mary's mouth for the remainder of Jesus' ministry. Only one other time is Mary mentioned in relation to Jesus' ministry. Even then He asked the rhetorical question, "Who is my mother; who are my brethren . . ." Biblical scholars assume—and I believe it is true—that Mary was constantly in the crowds surrounding her son. But she is not mentioned again until she stands at the cross.

Mary, like women of the harvest, had to see the glory of her son from God's perspective. As long as she perceived Him as her son, her natural relationship, she only placed pressure upon Him. Women must see their husbands, children, pastors, friends, etc., from God's perspective to help them reach their potential in God. Discernment is a matter of vision and perception. The *Nazareth mentality* always saw Jesus as *the carpenter's son*. Only God's perspective will release that supernatural power within someone's life.

Discernment means *waiting upon the Lord*. Discernment eliminates fretting because God will fulfill His promises to those who know how to wait upon Him in faith. Upon the cross, Jesus fulfilled His natural allegiance to Mary by saying, "John, behold your mother." How honorable Jesus was to her! She had once again become *Mother* because she knew her rightful place in His ministry.

Today so many women strive to be leaders in spiritual matters without understanding that God places *Esthers* and *Marys* according to His sovereign will, design and purposes. I believe that all women's spirits relate to some woman of Scripture. Some spirits are noble and godly, and some can be identified as destructive to the work of the Lord. Correction comes only by the Spirit of the Lord working in His Church to make ready the bride of Christ. God has no greater calling upon a Christian woman than for her to be identified as a *handmaiden of the Lord!*

MOVERS AND SHAKERS

Women are the motivators in the Kingdom of God. They are the movers and shakers who get things done! Women of harvest are a *new breed* in that they meet the challenges of this day in confidence. Women followed Jesus and supported Him. The Apostle Paul also mentions the women who ministered to him (Romans 16:1-6). Women become the support system of ministry for encouragement, intercession, discernment and confirmation. Financial support often comes to ministry from godly women, those recorded in Scripture and likewise from women in our day.

No woman is a better example of a *handmaiden* than Ruth. Her mother-in-law, Naomi, is a type of the Holy Spirit, and Ruth represents a type of the Church. First, allow me to say that too many women today identify with the role of Naomi more than with Ruth by attempting to *play Holy Spirit* in other people's lives. Such presumption always thwarts God's true plan by promoting error in human judgment and causing confusion in the Holy Spirit's direction.

Following Ruth's example, women of the harvest must listen to the instructions of the Holy Spirit

144

through God's Word, the Holy Spirit within them and the teaching of the five-fold ministry. First, Ruth was instructed by Naomi on how to be noticed (Ruth 2:19). To be the witness and standard of God's glory in the earth, women of the harvest must be noticed by the world in ways that are positive and honorable to the Lord. Jesus said that we are to be a "light upon a hill" which suggests great visibility. *Salt* is the flavor of ministry wherever God's people are. Christians must realize that we need to be noticed in order to take the gospel of the Kingdom around the world and to disciple all nations. The Holy Spirit will show us how to be noticed in a way that is unobtrusive and honorable to the Lord. But accept the fact that the Church has come into a time of great visibility—even through scandal—and visibility is necessary to God's plan for His Church in this hour. Don't expect the Church to ever retreat into the shadows as the *silent, sleeping giant* again. The cameras and microphones are pointed in our direction.

Secondly, Naomi instructed Ruth to stay close to Boaz. I can't overstate the importance of women of the harvest staying close to the men in this critical hour. Women must encourage men and undergird decisions of leaders with prayer within the Church in our day.

Ruth gleaned the fields of Boaz with the other maidens (Ruth 3:2). Women must also learn how to relate to other women of the harvest—to respect their callings without challenging or threatening them. Women need not only to move in the authority of their callings from God, but also to respect the lines of responsibility of other women moving in their particular callings. No woman is in competition with any other when she is in God's perfect will for her life.

Naomi recognized Ruth's need for security. Ironically, she instructed Ruth to find security by doing a very daring thing. Spending the night at Boaz's feet was a risk that Ruth took willingly. Undoubtedly her reputation was at stake. Notice that Boaz recognized that Ruth was known in the city as "a woman of excellence" (Ruth 3:10).

Boaz's acknowledgment of Ruth's good reputation stirred his protection of her. She left him in the morning "before one could recognize another" because following the leading of Naomi (the Holy Spirit) often involves *close intimacy* with the Lord. People of covenant meet the Lord in a secret place of close fellowship, under the wings of the Almighty (Psalm 91). Jesus said that things done in secret obedience to God such as fasting, giving to those in need or doing acts of kindness are rewarded openly.

The circumstances surrounding Ruth also involved timing (Ruth 4:7). Timing is a key ingredient of women of harvest. Proper timing requires keen sensitivity to the Holy Spirit's direction. Ruth had to wait for Boaz to follow proper procedures before God could bless her in becoming his wife (Ruth 4:7-12). So many women fail in this regard. Aggressiveness and anxiety are not of the Lord in a day when we need great power to witness effectively. God's timing is essential if we are to see His promises fulfilled.

Notice that Ruth did not grab onto a flesh relationship in an effort to find security (Ruth 4:10). God's plan is long-range, establishing His precepts and blessings for generations. Too many women sell out for immediate security before allowing their roots to go deep into the Lord as their eternal source. He is Jehovah-Jireh—the Provider. Security in the Lord always brings confidence, whereas flesh relationships are fleeting and empty.

Finally, Ruth is an example of faithfulness to women of the harvest. Ruth was faithful to Naomi, and then faithful to follow Boaz's instructions. God is calling today for *faithful, diligent laborers* in His harvest. The hours will seem long at times. Sometimes the field is full of rocks and we are asked to plow hard ground. At those times we must remember that sowing and reaping are absolute laws of God! Without exception, if we sow to the Spirit, we will reap life from the Spirit. The Apostle Paul said with firsthand knowledge of the difficult tasks of the harvest, "And let us not grow weary while doing good, for in due season [notice, timing again!], we shall reap if we do not lose heart" (Galatians 6:9).

So, who is she? Little girl? Seductress? Shrewd woman on the board of directors? Pastor in the pulpit? Glorified maid, chauffeur and cook? Or is she a comparable helpmeet in the work of the ministry?

Women of harvest! Arise! Shine! You have come to the Kingdom for such a time as this!

Chapter Six
Spiritual Trends

† The Church will discern the quality of life on earth by applying one question to all situations: *Who is in charge?*

† The Church will realize that the dream of our forefathers for a nation of liberty and justice is in jeopardy as never before.

† The Church has awakened to a crisis of public policy because legislation approves various types of immorality under the law.

† The Church will never again be silent or invisible in government's activities if we act responsibly now.

† The Church will see itself as God's agent in His government on earth, engaged in battle with satanic government. They will seek to influence civil government to serve the people.

† The Church will learn the difference between true authority and pseudo-authority.

† Good government will be defined according to biblical definitions of liberty and justice.

† The Church will realize its ministry as prophet, priest and king to fulfill its responsibility to government.

† The Church will address the same issues of quality living that Jesus addressed.

† The Church will use the additional resources available to it by the Holy Spirit to enable it to impact society for good.

6

GOD AND GOVERNMENT

" . . . **O**ne nation, under God, indivisible, with liberty and justice for all." These words resound across our land each day from the mouths of young children in public schools. Hands resting over their hearts, they stand at rapt attention, eyes fixed on the American flag. They have memorized the phrases they speak in unison.

They believe the truth of the words they are saying, though the definitions of *liberty* and *justice* are vague in their minds. The promises are noble. The declaration is idealistic. Children from every culture and ethnic origin stand together, shoulder to shoulder, proudly declaring the hopes of our forefathers over their land, their lives, their futures.

But what are the realities of those words? In all of our major cities, street people rummage through garbage cans to find food for the day. Crime steadily increases. Drug abuse has risen to epidemic proportions. Law enforcement officers are on the take. Politicians make deals under the table. Children are missing, while child pornography flourishes. The same schools which were racially integrated by busing in the sixties have now resegregated. The average American quickly admits that he feels less secure today in his own home than he did twenty years ago. Racial discrimination goes underground, then surfaces again in racial violence, job discrimination, segregated churches and Ku Klux Klan rallies.

And what of the words, ". . . under God . . .?" Prayer is illegal in American schools. One young man won a court injunction in Georgia which prevented hundreds of students from praying before their high school football games. Religious symbols of Christmas are banned from public buildings. The man on the street frowns as he looks into the television camera and answers the reporter's question with an angry cliche, "Religion and politics don't mix!" And humanists smile in agreement. Religion is suppressed under the law rather than protected by the distorted meaning of *separation of church and state.* One question determines the quality of life on planet earth: *Who is in charge?*

The contemporary Church has been reluctant until recently to address issues having to do with God and government or God *in* government. Christians have listened with respect to society's plea, "Don't mix politics and religion." Theirs seemed to be a reasonable request. We have refrained from becoming overbearing or aggressive in inflicting our Judeo-Christian values on the formation of public policy. Now we bear the consequences of our polite consideration: legalized abortion, humanistic curricula in education whose standards are in a steady decline, pornography shops and strip joints, legalized gambling, zoning laws against churches . . . the list is endless. Religious oppression flourishes under the law.

Conflicts of interest between Church and state have raged for centuries. Now in a permissive society with political unrest worldwide, the Church is pressed to address certain questions concerning morality and social order. We can be polite no longer. We have no choice. We have awakened to an explosion and have thrown down the luxuries of silence and passivity in the last seconds before it is too late. The reality of the scripture "faith without works is dead" has hit us squarely between the eyes. Unless we translate our convictions into the laws of our land, we will bear the blame for the loss of our precious freedom within a very brief span of years.

Survival of our civilization is the issue, and the Church is forced to speak at last. So how can the Church influence society and at the same time maintain independence from government? Even Christian activists ask, "How can the Church maintain objectivity concerning governmental spheres of authority?" The answers are found in the dream of our forefathers. We've gotten off course in the balance of politics and religion, but correction is imminent. The Constitution of the United States ensures that the Church maintain the liberty to serve as a conscience to society. Thank God, that day is here once again!

Quickly allow me to quiet the fears of people who

do not adhere to Judaism or Christianity by saying that no one is proposing a religious takeover of government. Forced worship of God is not worship. Our forefathers never intended for the Church to become the seat of government. Instead, the Church should represent the expression of God *in* government.

We must never forget that our ancestors left oppressive governments in their homelands to settle in North America. They hoped to maintain their religious liberties. They desired that their personal commitments to God would determine the quality of life they would know in the new world. Because of religious intolerance and unjust taxation, they prayed and dreamed of righteous rule—liberty and justice. They understood firsthand the proverb, "When the righteous are in authority, the people rejoice; But when a wicked man rules, the people groan" (Proverbs 29:2).

Nothing grieves the heart of God more than wicked leadership. He hears the cries of oppressed, helpless, hopeless people. They cry around the world today. The Spirit of God is opening the ears of the Church to hear and to respond to those cries by addressing three forms of government vying to be in control. Two of these governments are in head-to-head combat, and the other form of government is caught in the crossfire.

The government in the middle of a major war is civil government, an organism which is neither good nor bad in itself. In Scripture the body is compared to a temple under holy or unholy spiritual control, and civil government is somewhat like a flesh body in that regard. Whatever forces control a government—righteous or evil—determine the effects of that government's control in the lives of people.

THREE GOVERNMENTS

The Bible offers excellent examples of civil government as a guide to Christians in our response toward governmental policies. Interaction with civil government is inevitable for people who realize that they are stewards of their environment. Civil government has been given the charge to maintain safety and order. Idealistically, civil government is an extension of God's provision regarding the basic necessities of life for masses of people. The Old Testament representation of government is Pharaoh, and the New Testament refers repeatedly to Caesar.

Neither of these governments were godly, but they were directly influenced by God's people (representative of the Church today). Confrontations were numerous. Both governments realized the impact of God's people in the land and felt threatened by the bite of their spiritual messages. Their demands had teeth—large numbers of people in agreement and even supernatural intervention to ensure that they had the ear of the ruler. Both Pharaoh and Caesar were significantly limited in their jurisdiction over God's people. Through the cries of those people to God for righteousness and justice, both rulers were eventually destroyed for their stubborn resistance.

"He who rules over men must be just, ruling in the fear of God" (2 Samuel 23:3,4). Godly rulers warned their judges, "Take heed to what you are doing, for you do not judge for man but for the Lord, who is with you in the judgment. Now therefore, let the fear of the Lord be upon you; take care and do it, for there is no iniquity with the Lord our God, no partiality, nor taking of bribes" (2 Chronicles 19:6,7).

The second form of government is satanic government, a well-organized hierarchy of powers, principalities and rulers which is bent on conquest and destruction. This government exists in the spiritual realm, invisible and unrecognized by the majority of mankind. However, all feel the effects of this government's power.

The proponents of this government are becoming increasingly visible. The media have ridden the crest of interest in the supernatural by capitalizing on satanic forms of expression—astrology, witchcraft, seances, ghosts and goblins. People are spiritually hungry, and satanic government feeds them a tantalizingly unwholesome diet of unholy spirits. This government's faithful constituents are inevitably destroyed, either by power, wealth and fame or by drugs, sexual perversion or spiritual suicide.

Satanic government loves religion. Many religious, sincere people are its most useful citizens. They are adept at using the Bible to call evil things *good* and good things *evil*. For example, they have promoted as God's will a philosophy of looking to *another world* as a spiritual attitude, while leaving this world to become more and more corrupt. Scriptures such as "love not the world" are used to develop a monastic view of Christianity. Scriptures on the blessings of God are taken to extremes so that they promote greed by calling it *prosperity*. Division, judgment and strife are the fruits of religion in this government.

Satanic government is a military powerhouse engaged in fierce combat. Their opponents are becoming increasingly threatening because they have begun to realize the stakes of the war. Though history records remnants of Christians who understood the significance of the battle, only recently have mass numbers of Christians understood their identities as soldiers and their induction into God's army. The Apostle Paul understood the stakes and urged the Church to enter into training:

> Finally, my brethren, be strong in the Lord and in the power of His might. Put on the whole armor of God, that you may be able to stand against the wiles of the devil. For we do not wrestle against flesh and blood, but against principalities, against powers, against the rulers of the darkness of this age, against spiritual hosts of wickedness in the heavenly places. Therefore take up the whole armor of God, that you may be able to withstand in the evil day, and having done all, to stand. (Ephesians 6:10-13)

The third government is the government of God, Creator of all things. This government is eternal, unlike the other two governments which are confined to historical time. This government is called a Kingdom: the Kingdom of heaven, the Kingdom of God, the Kingdom of Christ. Though this government is invisible in its full manifestation, its commissioned agent on earth is the Church, an organism composed of spiritually born people from every nation which Scripture calls the body of Christ.

This Kingdom is built in covenant relationships between God and men from one generation to another. It is a Kingdom of righteousness, peace and joy. Citizens enter the Kingdom by faith in Jesus Christ. By faith, they experience a supernatural transfer of citizenship:

> He (God) has delivered us from the power of darkness and translated us into the kingdom of the Son of His love, in whom we have redemption through His blood, the forgiveness of sins. (Colossians 1:13,14)

Why is this Kingdom of peace and joy engaged in war? Why is this Kingdom so violently threatening to the goals of the other two kingdoms? Jesus Christ declared Himself to be the King of this Kingdom. Jesus said, "All authority has been given to Me in heaven and on earth . . ." (Matthew 28:18). He also instructed His Church to pray, ". . . Your Kingdom come. Your will be done on earth as it is in heaven . . ." (Matthew 6:10).

Immediately after the declaration that all authority has been given to Jesus, He instructed His Church to make disciples and to teach them (Matthew 28:19). This order is revolutionary. It ignites confrontation and bloodshed. The Church's mission is to bring God's authority to bear upon every aspect of life on planet earth. Agnostic and atheistic forces in the world intend to defeat that mission. World systems do not want God's influence in modern society, but still the Church is commissioned to speak boldly as the voice of Almighty God.

When we pray "Your Kingdom come," we are praying, "Let Your government in the heavenly realm come to manifestation in the earthly realm." If we are not pressing toward that goal, we fail to function as God's Church. The very moment we become so fearful or so intimidated that we declare that the Church should not be influencing the direction of civil government or confirming the defeat of satanic government, we cut off the work of the Holy Spirit.

GOD OR CAESAR?

The ultimate goal of the Holy Spirit on this planet is to manifest God's eternal reign in reality. Good civil government—ruling in righteousness and justice—will enable that reality to come about. The completed mission of the Church is the ultimate rule of God's government. Presently the Church must work diligently to manifest God's government as a prototype witness to the systems of this world. Christians are responsible to manifest the government of God's Kingdom, yet they are subjects in another government. That witness raises some very interesting questions:

> Then the Pharisees went and plotted how they might entangle Him in His talk. And they sent to Him their disciples with the Herodians, saying, "Teacher, we know that You are true, and teach the way of God in truth; nor do You care about anyone, for You do not regard the person of men. Tell us, therefore, what do You think? Is it lawful to pay taxes to Caesar, or not?" (Matthew 22:15-17)

The Pharisees were asking Jesus, "Should a religious, Judaistic society built in moral laws given by God pay taxes to Caesar, a worldly government?"

> But Jesus perceived their wickedness, and said, "Why do you test Me, you hypocrites? Show Me the tax money." So they brought Him a denarius. And He said to them, "Whose image and inscription is this?" They said to Him, "Caesar's." And He said to them, "Render therefore to Caesar the things that are Caesar's, and to God the things that are God's." (Matthew 22:18-21)

Which government holds our allegiance? It's a trick question that opens Christians to litigations repeatedly. Why did they question Jesus about loyalty to Caesar? Obviously, Jesus had already addressed the subject of government's responsibility. Jesus boldly addressed all of the pertinent issues of quality living which rubbed up against the laws of the land.

Jesus talked about the relationship of civil government to God's government. In the light of His previous remarks, Jewish leaders plotted to ensnare Jesus by His answers to their questions. These leaders wanted to bring Jesus under the indictment of the Law. They tried to get Him to establish His position so succinctly against civil government that Roman officials could arrest Him for promoting His revolution.

But Jesus did not answer them with a doctrinal statement. In the wisdom of God He asked them a question, "Whose image and inscription is on this coin?" Jesus tried to show them that whatever Caesar was doing for their good, they were responsible to finance. In other words, Christians need to finance garbage pickup, traffic lights, police protection, courthouse construction and maintenance, etc.

Jesus' answer did not establish a new doctrine. Jesus never advocated the separation of Church and state. He was simply answering a question. The question which they intended to be a trap for Him was simply, "Do we pay taxes to Caesar?" Man's financial responsibility to God was not relevant to this issue. The question was not, "Do we pay tithes to support God's government or pay taxes to support civil government?" They were not inquiring in terms of an *either/or* choice. They asked Jesus the trick question, "Do we (religious people) support the civil government?"

Often people misinterpret this passage of Scripture to say that Jesus established a premise for the separation of church and state. On the contrary, our nation has lost its proper sense of moral values because the Church fails to exert biblical influence upon the state. Two governments at war, satanic government and God's government, are both vying for influence over civil government. The laws of the land easily reveal who is winning the contest. At this point the visibility, declaration and power of the Church becomes mandatory if we are to turn the tide before it is too late!

A WARNING

I am not a fearmonger; I am a messenger of hope. But if Christians do not respond to the alarming direction of laws governing our humanistic society, within the next twenty-five years the United States of America will fall in total moral corruption and social devastation. People will starve. Our money will be useless. We will go the way of many other nations in which the state is god, while God's true voice is silenced by law under a penalty of imprisonment and death. Are Christians hearing God's warnings, His direction for us in this hour? How does God speak to His Church today? Some Christians argue that spiritual authority has moved from the pulpit to a majority rule by people sitting in the pew. I totally disagree. I contend that God has placed His authority of direction in the pulpit and in the callings of the five-fold ministry.

The Teacher of truth (the Holy Spirit) ministers through various callings He has set forth in the Church (Ephesians 4). To the degree that the body of Christ hears and responds to God's direction, God's government becomes authoritative in the world today. The Word of God is preached, then the body of believers implements God's Word in their lives and thereby influences social order. However, if the Word of God is not properly taught from the pulpit, God's direction can never reach people sitting in the pews

161

of the Church. Philip asked the eunuch if he understood the Scriptures. The eunuch replied, "How can I, unless someone guides me?" (Acts 8:31). In forty-three years of ministry I have never felt a greater urgency to address the distinctions between God's government and civil government than now. I am not alone in recognizing the urgency of the Holy Spirit in taking this message to Christians while the doors are still open for us to make a difference. How do we bring God's Kingdom, God's thoughts, into human experience? How do we bring God's government into a spiritual realm to influence civil government?

In the beginning the earth was without form and void. A chaotic condition had disrupted order on our planet. God's purpose from the dawn of creation was to establish Jesus Christ and His Church to restore order in the earth. That plan necessitates civil government until the witness to God's government is completed in human history. Maintaining peace and order for the witness of the gospel of the Kingdom to go forth is the primary purpose of civil government. Somehow many Christians have reached the false conclusion that civil government is always oppressive to the cause of God's government. No, civil government is necessary for now.

Recently in a television news interview I was asked whether I opposed television evangelists' appearing before a Senate committee investigating their finances. I answered the reporter, "Why should men and women of God be afraid of civil servants' questioning them? We are 'the people.' We are 'the government.' "

The Church has a responsibility to influence government by preaching and teaching God's Word.

Christian senators and governors need to recognize their callings to maintain peace and order, both as public servants and as members of the Church representing God's government. A minister's role is primarily to influence a congregation so that as Christians rise to positions of influence in secular society, they hear God's clear direction for governing people under laws of righteousness and justice. When Jesus said that He had been given *all authority,* we must recognize that even unjust governments are under His command.

> Let every soul be subject to the governing authorities. For there is no authority except from God, and the authorities that exist are appointed by God. Therefore whoever resists the authority resists the ordinance of God, and those who resist will bring judgment on themselves. For rulers are not a terror to good works, but to evil. Do you want to be unafraid of the authority? Do what is good, and you will have praise from the same. For he is God's minister to you for good. But if you do evil, be afraid; for he does not bear the sword in vain; for he is God's minister, an avenger to execute wrath on him who practices evil. (Romans 13:1-4)

No authority exists except from God—whether it be governmental, educational, social or economical. All proper authority governs with principles established by the laws of God's government. Rulers governing for the good of mankind are assigned by God. Good government always protects the welfare of mankind. Oppressive government is pseudo-authority. It will not last because satanic government ultimately destroys all under its influence. Pseudo-authority is always short-lived.

Mammon is a god of satanic government which

has gripped the affairs of civil government in a seemingly inextricable stronghold. Because government over-spending and the voluminous national debt are such hot political issues, please allow me to comment on the contentions of civil government toward the finances of God's government.

Since politicians are elected to serve the good of our society, we pay taxes to enable them to function. Ironically, society warns the Christian community, "You had better investigate where your Church dollars are going!" Too often citizens do not know where their tax dollars are spent! We have a responsibility to ensure that our taxes go to civil systems working to provide quality living.

When government tears down the worth of individuals, destroys wholesome family values and divides people from one another, we need to say, "Listen, government! You are failing to be rulers for good. As God's Church, we call you to task!" If government officials do not promote quality living, they are not of God. The Church must not sit idly by and allow evil rulers to set the social agenda. Their authority is motivated by greed for power. Eventually they will fall, and we will fall with them.

Those men and women who war against the function of good government are working in accordance with satanic government. Those forces presently control world systems. The enemy comes to steal, to kill and to destroy (John 10:10). Good government will never steal, kill or destroy human lives or the quality living which is founded on biblical values—love, peace, joy, thanksgiving, encouragement. The future of our world rests upon our understanding of the principles that were the dream of our forefathers, the self-evident truths of *life, liberty and the pursuit of happiness.*

Good government will not steal character, human dignity, equal opportunities, the rewards of the work ethic, free enterprise, the right to own property, healthy self-images for all ethnic and racial minorities, the right to raise children according to loving parental consciences. Good government will not kill the right to open expression in our society. It will not kill the ability to implement that which God calls us to perform—the demonstration of the benefits of quality living.

If civil government tears down any of these freedoms, it ceases to be good government. It ceases to operate under the blessings of God's government. Allow me to give an illustration from Scripture to clarify the criteria of good government:

Two apostles were arrested and thrown into prison by governmental officials for preaching and healing in the name of Jesus Christ. In the middle of the night, an angel opened the prison doors and said to them,

> "Go, stand in the temple and speak to the people all the words of this life." And when they heard that, they entered the temple early in the morning and taught. But the high priest and those with him came and called the council together, with all the elders of the children of Israel, and sent to the prison to have them brought. (Acts 5:20,21)

Governmental officials found the apostles preaching in the temple and brought them before the civil council. They asked them the question, "Did we not strictly command you not to teach in this name? And look, you have filled Jerusalem with your doctrine, and intend to bring this Man's blood on us!" The apostles were imprisoned because they were preaching abundant living through Jesus Christ. Their message was a direct confrontation to the motivations of civil law—in this case to keep people from knowing truth.

> Then Peter and the other apostles answered and said "We ought to obey God rather than men . . ." (Acts 5:29)

In essence, Peter replied, "When man's government contradicts God's government, we must obey God." That answer addresses the issue of who is in control. If civil government opposes quality living, we must obey God's government instead. The central issues of government focus upon choices between being controlled by a humanistic state or being covered by a God-fearing government. Are we going to enjoy a society that advocates godly morality and biblical truths, or will we have a humanistic society legislating against God's Word, protecting the lawbreaker and condoning immorality in the formation of public policy? That is the central issue, the choice we must make quickly.

Secular society trembles when a man proclaims, "I have heard from God!" Such a statement causes an onslaught of criticism and sets off alarms in the humanistic press. If the Bible is merely a book confined to the library shelf, biblical truths pose absolutely no threat to humanistic ideologies. But when the Book is opened and read, the Holy Spirit quickens human understanding. The Spirit of God begins to release power in human circumstances. Suddenly, worldly authorities attack with venom. God's Word always challenges world systems that in any way impede the liberty of mankind or enslave the Spirit of abundant living.

THE CHURCH IN SOCIETY

The ministry of Jesus Christ provides the example for the ministry of the Church in the world. First, Jesus spoke as a prophet. The Church must also speak prophetically. Jesus was the greatest prophet of all. A prophetic voice always proclaims God's will. Jesus said, "You have heard . . . but I say to you . . ." (Matthew 5:27,28). It is very important to understand Jesus' role as a prophet, so that likewise the Church proclaims God's Word and brings God's thoughts to people who have *ears to hear* on planet earth. A church which fails to speak prophetically functions only as a social institution because it lacks purpose and direction.

Second, Jesus Christ ministered in the role of a priest. Likewise the Church brings healing and help to hurting people. Priests stand as mediators to reconcile man and God. The priest says, "Your sins are forgiven." The priestly ministry in the Church brings sinners to the Table of the Lord. Communion with God restores man through forgiveness of sins. Restoration results in healing, strength and direction for people's lives.

Jesus said to a paralytic man, "Your sins are forgiven." The scribes looked on thinking, "This Man blasphemes." But Jesus, knowing their thoughts, said to them, "Which is easier, to say to the paralytic, 'Your sins are forgiven you,' or to say, 'Arise, take up your bed and walk'?" (Mark 2:9). As in Jesus' ministry, the Church serves as God's priest in a world that needs forgiveness and healing.

Third, Jesus Christ is a king. The Church, assuming this ministry, will face social confrontations. God's Word says, "the government will be upon His

167

shoulder" (Isaiah 9:6). Jesus Christ was born a king, the ultimate authority of all governments. As long as Jesus ministered only as a prophet and a priest, He wasn't a threat to civil government, and even satanic government tolerated Him. But when Jesus stood before Pilate, the ruler asked Him that fatal question, "Are you a king?" Jesus' answer meant that the cross was only hours away.

Don't be fooled. World systems do not want to be subject to the authority of God's government. That is the reason men such as Martin Luther King, Jr. die violent deaths. Whenever a man insists that God's justice must determine the policies of government, he is on a path to prison or assassination.

Christians can lay hands on the sick or pray prayers in the Church without inciting too much interference, but the minute Christian beliefs begin to impact social policy, we must expect violent confrontations. Once a minister says to the media, "God has spoken! What the government is doing is not of God!" I promise that pastor will face character assassination. All issues on this planet filter down to one basic question, *"Who is in charge?"* When the ministries of prophet, priest and king function properly in the Church, we maintain both social order and an anointed flow of ministry. In the ideal balance between the governments of Church and state, society views the Church as its source of help. But when the Church ceases to minister in its total calling as prophet, priest and king, it ceases to have any reason to exist.

THE CHURCH AGAINST INJUSTICE

Injustices toward innocent people made Jesus angry. Those same injustices which incensed Christ must also anger the Church. Any laws enslaving mankind should ignite the Church's anger. Any laws battling against family stability should also anger the Church. Anything that brings threats of violence to communities should move the Church to action. Any laws that set one segment of society against another in prejudice should make the Church take a bold stand. Any laws that demean or belittle human worth from the cradle (including the womb) to the grave should mobilize the Church to defend those who are oppressed.

God is saying "I will build my Church and hell won't stop it." The Church is beginning to realize a tremendous move of the Holy Spirit on this planet. With increasing momentum, we are beginning to see the manifestation of the Kingdom of God impact civil government for the first time since our forefathers recorded their dream in words that school children recite. The satanic government is alarmed. No wonder the spirit of Belshazzar trembles as he sits on his throne. His knees should be knocking together (Daniel 5). The Holy Spirit, working through His Church, will bring down the powers of evil in this world.

The Word of the Lord always divides and separates the counterfeit from the real. The Word of God is quick and powerful and sharper than a two-edged sword. It exposes the intents of the heart as people make choices. Unbelievers have no problem with God's reign in heaven as long as it remains in heaven. Problems arise when God's authority impacts planet earth.

In order to determine the areas of injustice toward which the Church's energy should be channeled, examine the life of Jesus to see what He advocated in social change. These things made Jesus angry:

1. *Jesus was angered at abuses in the house of God.* He was angry when people were being deceived in the house of worship. Merchandising to buy sacrifices had replaced worship. We should become angry when the Church fails to address the needs of people, fails to provide spiritual food that gives strength for living.

2. *Jesus was angered at those who blasphemed against the Holy Spirit* (Matthew 12:31-34). Jesus called religious leaders *vipers* because they attacked the work of the Holy Spirit. Blasphemy against the Holy Spirit simply means failing to yield to the work of the Holy Spirit. Jesus said, "When He, the Spirit of truth, has come, He will guide you into all truth . . ." (John 16:13). Jesus was angry at the accusation that He was working under the power of Satan. Such accusations are blasphemous.

3. *Jesus became angry when any leaders placed heavy burdens upon the people following them.* Jesus became angry with governments that placed heavy burdens upon people, preventing them from enjoying abundant living. Today in the United States, it is almost impossible for a couple earning an average income to buy a house. Something is wrong with an economy in which people who need houses the most cannot afford them. People work long hours merely to exist, then they are forced to earn additional income from a second job. Something is wrong with that sort of economy. Jesus was angry with people who placed heavy burdens upon others instead of setting them free.

4. *Jesus became angry when leaders of the people shut the door to the Kingdom of God.* These leaders include officials. They prevent implementation of the

Kingdom of God in human circumstances. Jesus said to leaders of the people, "You shut up the kingdom of heaven against men; for you neither go in yourselves, nor do you allow those who are entering to go in" (Matthew 23:13). Widows struggled in hopeless circumstances. Any government placing widows and orphans—single parents—in distress is not a government of God. Any government that protects the criminal with laws sanctioning criminal activity that abuses widows and orphans is not a government ordained of God. Jesus was angry when He said, ". . . You pay tithe . . . and have neglected the weightier matters of the law: justice and mercy and faith . . ." (Matthew 23:23). Anytime these three virtues are not governing the order of society, the Church should become angry.

Jesus said to leaders, ". . . I send you prophets . . . some of them you will kill and crucify . . ." (Matthew 23:34). Religious leaders would not listen to the prophets and they silenced their voices. The underlying motive for government calling men of God in for questioning is usually an attempt to kill their influence. Someone argues, "They should not be afraid of questioning." I agree, but let us be honest.

The true motive for investigating the Church is to kill prophetic voices. Something is wrong when civil government advocates freedom of speech, and yet spends its time investigating the normal activities of the Church. What about the proven abuses of ministers who are deceptive? Should not people be protected from them? God is big enough to judge His own affairs and protect the innocent whose motives are pure. Deception is always judged in the house of God. Elders rule in those matters. When accusations against the Church are continuously publicized by the secular media, the Church must be defensive and cannot move forward in ministry. I think it is ironic that the government is investigating the financial affairs of the Church.

Christians need to write congressmen and ask them how much investigations of evangelists cost the taxpayers. Find out how many of our tax dollars are spent by governmental officials for travel and entertainment while they prepare questions on where the Church is spending its contributions. Ask representatives why they are spending our money on trips abroad under the guise of *official government business*. How many fact-finding trips do they take around the world at the taxpayers' expense?

Investigating Church finances is a distraction from over-spending in the national economy. Officials want us to concentrate on financial abuses in the Church. Where Christian people might have mismanaged one dollar, thousands and thousands of Church dollars educate children, minister to the sick, feed the hungry, give hope to the dying. It is time for Christians to stand up and say boldly, "Government, get out of our business!"

Now that we have examined the abuses that made Jesus angry, I will list five injustices that should make the Church angry and mobilize us to action.

1. *Anything that enslaves mankind in spirit, mind or body.* I have no problem with people worshiping God quietly, but it is no one's business if I shout before the Lord! Anything that enslaves the minds of men leaves them in ignorance. Any form of government that leaves people ignorant, including an educational system which offers so few solutions to illiteracy, is not of God. Why don't we find out

where educational dollars are going?

Is the Church affecting the quality of life in America? Are Christians content to blame poor government for our social and educational problems? We point fingers toward government while churches and ministers need to be the ones saying, "We know the source of solutions. We are the ones responsible for good government."

The Church should be angry at any forces intimidating the body, such as addiction to drugs. I believe that if government seriously addresses the drug traffic in the United States, it can be stopped. Here is another area in which God's government has sat back and allowed satanic government to put society to sleep. Christians are accountable to God for such an atrocity as the drug traffic facing our children in the halls of public schools each day. Isn't it time we did something about it?

Jesus saw a lady bowed low who could not straighten up. He said to her, "Woman, you are loosed from your infirmity." She stood up straight. The ruler of the synagogue said to the onlooking crowd that Jesus should heal on one of the six days of the week but not on the Sabbath. Jesus replied with a very key statement, ". . . Ought not this woman being a daughter of Abraham . . . be loosed?" (Luke 13:16). Forces that adversely affect the body should make the Church angry.

2. *The Church must become angry at anything that can destroy the family.* Any government that establishes a philosophy that causes the family to suffer is not a government of God. The most basic human government in the world is the family unit. Any policy that fails to assist a family in maintaining health and stability is destructive to the social

173

order. For example, some aspects of our welfare system, such as giving advantages to unwed mothers, destroy the family instead of knitting it together. Ironically, tax laws discriminate against married couples.

Our government allows subversive behavior in our streets. Who challenges a government that cannot control human behavior in the streets of our cities? Any government that does not address the safety and preservation of its citizens causes the downfall of the nation.

3. *The Church must become angry at anything that instigates confusion, chaos or anarchy in order to disrupt the social order.* A spirit of criticism quickly becomes a conspiracy as others join ranks. Conspiracy leads to anarchy. Such spirits of criticism and accusation have been unleashed in our nation today that anarchy is inevitable unless Christians pray diligently and speak boldly to the issues. Christian elders who understand restoration and the compassion of God must step to the forefront and silence the accusers.

Few men and women of courage will escape personal attacks for speaking out. In spite of the personal risks and the problems, Christians must move forward in the righteousness and power of Jesus Christ to speak God's direction to our society.

4. *The Church should become angry when one segment of society is set against another with division and strife.* Any kind of prejudice preventing people from coming into spiritual unity for good should anger the Church. No segregated group, black or white, rich or poor, male or female exists in God's government. Any civil government that does not promote unity and equal opportunity is not a govern-

ment blessed of God.

5. *The Church should be angry at anything that demeans personal dignity.* Ambition, pride or lust wars against the principle of love by demeaning other people. We are granted the right under our Constitution to live and die as we choose under the auspices of the law. When laws demean quality living for the unborn, or for the aged, someone must become their advocate. The Church must protect those who are unable to speak for themselves.

What can Christians do to ensure social order and peace? Four lepers sat dying at the gate of Samaria. One finally had enough insight to ask a question, "Why are we sitting here until we die . . .?" (2 Kings 7:3). The answer to that question would seem to be obvious! Wouldn't you think it would be obvious that a government in trouble would ask, "Why do we sit here until we die"? Isn't it time for Christians to take notice? Time is running out!

We must rouse ourselves and say, "We are not going to allow our families to die! We are not going to allow our liberties to die! We have fought around the world to preserve freedom! We will not allow our rights to be taken away by poor government!"

SO WHAT CAN CHRISTIANS DO?

The Church must become the manifestation of God's government in society. The Church matures to become a comparable bride to the person and ministry of Jesus Christ by hearing and doing the things Jesus taught and did. *The mature body of Christ will be decisive.* She must no longer be tossed to and fro in decisions, but be able to make up her mind and implement God's will.

The Church must be discerning. Discernment

175

comes by applying God's Word in practical ways. Discernment marks the maturity of the Church.

The Church must have determination. We cannot grow weary in well doing. The woman who went again and again to the unrighteous judge did not receive her request because of who she was, but because of her persistence (Luke 18:2-5). Diligence, discipline, fortitude are all qualities that Christians must ask the Holy Spirit to give them. Let the weak say, "I am strong!"

If we as Christians are going to live as *salt* and *light* in our society, we must do more than merely register to vote. Secular society also votes. God's government calls the Church to exercise responsibility as citizens which secular society cannot do.

The world does not have prayer power. God can pull down the strongholds of Satan by the prayer power of the Church.

The world cannot use the keys of the Kingdom (Matthew 16:19). The world operates with limited authority, but only the Church has the keys to eternity. Only the Church can bind and loose power in heavenly places. These are workable tools and weapons for conquest that God has given only to His people.

We have the Holy Spirit to empower us. The power struggles between God's government, satanic government and civil government will be settled by the miraculous intervention of God (1 Kings 18:20-40). As we grow in maturity, God can trust us with His miraculous power. God is waiting for the demonstration of a mature Church so that He can impart His power to speak to adverse winds, blinded eyes, deaf ears. God's gifts will not be given only to an individual, but the gift of healing, for example, will flow through the body of Christ. The Spirit of the Lord will move upon the people of God to grant them strength and long life because of their obedience.

As the Spirit of the Lord moves in the house of God, people will have exceptional wisdom and insight. The Holy Spirit, Who is the wisdom of God, will be imparted at a level never known before. Businesses committed to God will discover ways and means to solve financial problems that the world has been unable to resolve.

We have prayer power, power that comes from the Holy Spirit. We have the keys to the Kingdom. Most importantly, remember the example of Jesus as we war against evil powers and authorities around us. His authority brings all of creation under the rule of God. Don't apologize for proclaiming that Jesus Christ is King of kings and Lord of lords. Jesus is not only King over the Church; He is King over the world, over all creation. And we are the heirs of the world through Jesus Christ.

The Church must assume responsibility for social order and influence upon legislation as never before. Love is the strategy. God's Word, the example of Jesus Christ's life, ministry and character, serves as our standard. Our strongest witness rests in a lifestyle based on biblical truth and Kingdom principles. Let us be bold as we follow the leading of the Holy Spirit.

Chapter Seven
Spiritual Trends

† The Church will be forced to address the imminent threat of destruction of the United States of America.

† The primary issue of contention is based upon belief in the origin and value of human life.

† The Church will offer guidance on three questions determining quality of life: Who is in charge? Who owns or possesses this object or land that I want? How can I find happiness and security in relationships?

† The Church will address modern, social upheaval caused by the lust of the flesh, the lust of the eyes and the pride of life.

† Satan will continue trying to offer people shortcuts to abundant living.

† Satan will confuse people's reasons for living.

† An attack will continue against biblical foundations of truth and justice.

† An attack will continue against our system of training by disregarding history, art and culture and focusing on nonessentials.

† Society will be overrun with people who have confused their priorities.

† The lack of trust will continue to undermine authority in society, government, the Church and the family.

† An attack will continue against any sense of eternity.

† Belief in the metaphysical and miraculous will continue to be viewed with scorn by many people in society.

† Christians will regain the voice they have lost through years of division and complacency.

† Conservative politics and Christianity will become more and more distinct from one another.

† The Church will secure the future by learning how to release the Holy Spirit.
† The Church will learn to use the keys of the Kingdom in spiritual warfare.
† The Church will learn to make intercession with Jesus Christ.
† The Church will learn the meaning of being personal overcomers.
† The Church will learn to move in a spirit of unity.
† All citizens will be pressed into making spiritual choices determining the quality of life in their nation and for their families' futures.

7

TO KILL AN EAGLE

The eagle was chosen as the emblem for the United States because it represents vision and power. No bird can soar more majestically than an eagle—yet hundreds of feet above ground he can spot the smallest rodent. No bird can match the thrust of the eagle's wings in the sky. The eagle represents qualities of strength that are unsurpassed—qualities the United States of America has also represented in upholding the cause of freedom around the world.

Recently as I watched a movie about the fall of a great dynasty in China, the Spirit of the Lord spoke to me that we are living in the days of the "killing of an eagle; the killing of the United States of America." For many reasons I resist delivering such a grave warning as this. Yet I am compelled to expose the imminent threat over our lives and the future of our children's lives while there is still time.

First allow me to say that I do not believe that the United States is God's only nation in the world representing the cause of justice and liberty. We have made many mistakes historically which we cannot justify. We have known many national failures in social action, in foreign affairs, in legislation. So I am not waving *Old Glory* in unrestrained national pride.

I do contend, however, that the origins and purposes of this nation that our forefathers espoused were ordained by God. The inalienable rights stated in the preamble of our Constitution are basic principles of the Christian message. The concepts of man's personal worth were emphasized in formulating the foundational laws of this land. Our founding fathers were sensitive to the issues of freedom because they were dedicated to ensuring quality living for themselves and their posterity.

I would even contend that the last vestige of man's freedom protected by government rests in the free nations of the earth. The United States certainly stands among those free nations in a power struggle against oppressive governments who disregard individual rights. We are seen among the nations of the world as a bulwark of freedom, an example of an open society which protects the rights to free speech and equal opportunities.

So what is the basis of the power struggle we face? One side believes that an individual is created by God and has certain rights to enjoy quality living as a human being. The other side charges that the state controls human life. The only value of a human being is whatever that person's value becomes in corporate society for the benefit of the state.

Three questions determine every human being's quality of life: Who is in charge of my life? Who owns or possesses an object, a piece of land, etc., that I want? How can I find happiness and security in relationships? These questions constantly test our basic values as to how we fulfill our inner longings and find meaning in life.

To answer these three basic questions of life an individual will sacrifice, go to any extreme, work endlessly, plot both long-term and short-term strategies and endure hardships. In order to be in control, to own something of value, to have a desirable relationship, people will plan endlessly to achieve their goals. Education, insurance, security measures, financial planning, joining organizations, all of these are motivated by the desire to meet basic needs. Some people will even resort to killing, stealing and lying to ensure that their needs are met.

THREE BASIC DRIVES

The Bible categorizes three basic human drives, calling them the lust of the flesh, the lust of the eyes and the pride of life (1 John 2:16-17). *Flesh* is neither good nor bad, but the motivation of flesh determines good or evil actions. Basic human drives motivate actions which can yield either destructive or constructive results. Motivations for actions are extremely important in determining the rippling effects of those actions upon oneself, one's family, one's community, one's nation, etc.

The lust of the flesh pertains to appetites. Having appetites is normal and is neither good nor bad.

All people get hungry, thirsty and have emotional and sexual desires. But we live in a society wrecked by uncontrolled appetites—cocaine, alcohol, tobacco, sexual addictions, aberrated lifestyles. People have totally lost control of their desires. Chemicals control them. They are in bondage to feelings—emotional highs and lows. Whatever it takes to get there, people will do. Anything that takes away individual choices ultimately becomes an evil force with the potential of destroying all of mankind.

The lust of the eyes pertains to desires. The Bible speaks of desires in a positive way—the desires of our hearts. Simply having desires within our hearts is not evil. But when the eyes look upon objects and want to possess them, a person can lose control over his desires. Then desires begin to control him.

Covetousness becomes a chain locking millions of people into bondage. Whatever it takes to own whatever they want, they are willing to do. People work overtime, take extra jobs, live in debt, lie, cheat, steal—all to possess the things their eyes have seen and desired. Television, the movie industry and advertisers have created techniques for controlling great numbers of people through the lust of the eyes.

The pride of life pertains to who is in charge. Leadership is not evil, but a lust to be in control is one of the most destructive motivations that a person can experience. Pride is synonymous with vanity. People want to be the ones making the decisions, the ones controlling situations. This motivation produces workaholics, social climbers and cutthroat businessmen. Power is the commodity. Some people will kill to prove their point and get their way. They will trample others to get ahead.

Not only are the results of these basic drives destroying our society, but examples of their destruction are also demonstrated repeatedly as warnings throughout Scripture. In the Garden of Eden, Eve looked upon the forbidden fruit and saw that it was good to the eye. She wanted the fruit for herself. She saw that it was good to eat—the lust of the flesh. The serpent told Eve that when she ate the fruit, she would be like God—the pride of life. Eve's deception and Adam's sin began the curse of these drives in the lives of all mankind.

The most drastic contrast to the scene in the Garden of Eden is lived out on the mountain of temptation. There Jesus faced Satan's lies in direct confrontation. Jesus was a man with all the basic drives of manhood. He felt the same temptations we feel. But whereas the first Adam sinned, the last Adam was victorious over the drives of self-centered manhood.

After fasting for forty days Jesus resisted the temptation to turn stones into bread in order to satisfy His flesh. Jesus answered Satan that man does not live by a satisfied appetite, but by obedience to God's voice. Did Satan admit his defeat then? Oh, no!

Upon the pinnacle of the temple, Satan flattered Jesus by telling Him that God would not allow Him to be harmed if He would cast Himself down. In essence, Satan told Jesus that God would take care of His flesh because He was an exception to other men. Jesus replied, "But it is written, 'Tempt not the Lord your God.' " Jesus resisted pride, vanity and expecting exceptional treatment from God. So many Christians today think of themselves as *exceptions* to every rule!

Finally, Satan took Jesus to the highest moun-

185

tain (always representing authority in the Word of the Lord). Jesus looked upon the world as Satan offered all of it to Him if He would simply bow down and worship him. Jesus saw enticing possessions, felt the surge of power, knew He could know instant satisfaction to any of the longings of His manhood. Then He answered, "There is only one God, and I will not bow to you, Satan."

Consider the contrast of these two scenes. The nature of the first Adam and of the last Adam reside in every born again believer. Which nature rules? We decide this rulership in every decision of life. Are we motivated by what looks good? Feels good? Tastes good? Do we insist on having what we want regardless of whom it hurts or what the consequences are? Must we be in charge? Must we have our own way?

The answers to these questions bring us either to freedom in God or to bondage in fulfilling our own desires. One nature transforms us into light—goodness, gentleness, meekness, truth, love and trust. The other nature enslaves us to a counterfeit form of authority. People do not even realize that they are following satanic decrees. They may even go to church, but they make choices in life based upon their greed and selfish desires. Those choices become the price of freedom for ourselves and our children. And the time for us to enjoy making choices is running out.

Satan offers us shortcuts to abundant living. He tries to make us believe that lying, stealing, killing, taking drugs and forcing people to do whatever we want them to do will bring fulfillment. We must have the most powerful bombs and weapons and be the biggest kid on the block. We must be in charge. We must have so much control that we exert the least amount of effort possible to make others do whatever we want. The gang mentality translates into easy power and controlling other people's lives by intimidating them.

No wonder people are not making covenants with God nor with one another. We want shortcuts to fulfillment—not commitments for the long haul. I believe that every cell of our bodies is driven by these destructive forces. Wants. Desires. Lusts. These drives are resident within us. "Who is going to be in charge? How am I going to own this? Where is the person who can give me happiness and security?" We battle over these questions in our bodies, in our families, in our nation.

As I began to think about *the killing of an eagle,* I saw clearly a strategy of Satan and his cohorts to destroy America. *Killing an eagle* means killing insight and vision. On our present course, within two decades we will see a total disintegration of our national government. A new form of government will emerge which will totally disregard individual rights. Here is the strategy:

HOW TO KILL AN EAGLE

To kill an eagle, Satan confuses people as to their reasons for living. Spiritual understanding is darkened while people live to satisfy their appetites. Property rights mean nothing to people who are addicted to cocaine. When society's appetites are out of control, tyranny reigns. People are ripe for revolution. They reason, "Why worry about tomorrow? Live for today! Who cares about the lives of our children! What about us now!"

Another way to kill an eagle is to destroy the foundations of abundant living. Undermine the family as being the core of society. Use television to flood the family rooms of America every night with immorality, vanity and fantasy. Destroy communication among family members. Distort family values of personal caring to focus on an accumulation of gross materialism. Destroy moral values with a Hollywood concept of sexuality without commitment.

Meanwhile, governmental foundations are also being destroyed. Killing the eagle means disregarding the principles of justice and freedom that are the guidelines in the formation of our laws. The Bill of Rights and the Constitution are considered to be antiquated. Old-fashioned values are considered to be worthless. The courts are for the benefit of the criminal's rights. The elderly of our land are regarded as only standing in the way of progress—problems to deal with.

The third way to kill an eagle is to destroy our system of training. Corrupt education by consuming students' hours of preparation for life with nonessential information. Ignore basic instruction in reading, writing and mathematics. Offer shortcuts to education which do not require discipline. Offer easy methods instead of challenges. Within one generation, the enlightenment of centuries can be totally lost.

Subjects such as art, history and music are considered to be nonessential information to those trying to destroy a generation. How can people possibly live quality lives without a sense of their heritage? It cannot be done. They are too shortsighted in their goals and in their understanding of humanity.

I also agree with the slogan, "Those who read, lead." Anyone believing that videos can replace reading does not understand the psychological and physiological processes of the mind. Watching a movie is a passive mental activity compared to the active mental process of reading a book on the same subject. Reading requires imagination and concentration for comprehension. Indeed, readers are leaders! Anyone discouraging our children from reading is paving the way for them to be ruled by others. Reading is one way to assure personal freedom more than any other skill because it becomes a mental escape and a source of solutions to any problem. Books contain the wisdom of the ages.

The fourth way to kill an eagle is to confuse priorities of life. Make sports a god. Make status living the ultimate goal in life. Make people worship beauty and pursue it. Make ownership and possessions determine one's value as a human being.

Make entertainment a god so that people spend money they don't have without hesitation only to amuse themselves for a few hours or a few days. Control people's time and schedules so that they are always hurrying, doing absolutely nonessential activities. Press people into vanity so that they waste money and time and feel as if they have accomplished something when they are exhausted from worthless pursuits.

The fifth way to kill an eagle is to destroy trust wherever it exists. Unleash judgmentalism in society. Concentrate on religious judgments which override any principles of grace and mercy. Commission investigators dedicated to exposing any flaws in the conduct or character of Christian teachers or people in authority.

Unleash suspicion in society so that people look at one another and say, "What is your angle? What are you up to? What do you really want?" Focus on unearthing details that make people feel worthless or guilty. Spread darkness so that no one knows who is in charge. Create an atmosphere of chaos so that any semblance of order within society is destroyed or rejected by the masses.

The sixth way to kill an eagle is to take away any sense of eternity. Let people live with an attitude of "eat, drink and be merry for tomorrow we may die—and after death is nothing at all!" Take away any hope beyond the grave. Make people believe that nothing they do really makes any difference. A lack of eternity will not only destroy hope, but also all accountability for one's actions.

Finally, the seventh way to kill an eagle is to destroy any belief in metaphysical, miraculous power. Insist that people give credibility only to natural understanding. Any reference to the metaphysical should only be in connection with New Age thinking or the occult. Make science a god. Extol intellect and ridicule any occurrence that cannot be explained through scientific or reasonable explanations.

By taking away belief in miracles, the message of salvation is lost. The new birth is the greatest miracle of all—greater than stretching forth a withered arm, healing a blinded eye or a lame foot. The greatest miracle of all is the confidence to say, "I know that Jesus Christ died for my sins and I am made over again because of Him." Salvation is eternal. When eternal values are lost, tyranny reigns in a society.

We are forced into confrontations against the strategy to kill an eagle—our freedom, our nation. This strategy is intended to close the doors of our open society. This strategy is working quickly in our nation today. Some will awaken to the urgency of this hour, and others will sleep peacefully until they are devoured upon their beds.

THE DAY THE MUSIC DIED

God's spokesmen warned Christians in Russia, in Cuba, in Poland. Will Christians in America hear the word of the Lord? Will we hear God's warning only when the wall is built or the curtain is drawn? Will we be arguing over the color of drapes and vestments and which hymns to sing while tyrants take control of our government? How much longer will we walk the streets of our land in freedom, speak what we want to speak, assemble whenever we decide, choose our leaders and worship in freedom?

There is a song by secular prophet Don McLean called, *American Pie* that poetically describes ". . . the day the music died," the death of the American dream. The lyrics of that song are frightfully chilling in their implications, yet now we live so close to the total reality of those words. How free are we to dream, and to make our dreams become reality? What freedoms have we already lost while we were rocked to sleep by complacency? How free will our children be in twenty-five years to experience life, liberty and the pursuit of happiness?

If you are old enough to remember life in the 50's, the *Happy Days* era, then you can understand the harsh contrast of life in our country today compared with only a few decades ago. I don't mean to glorify *the good 'ol days*, because we had our share of problems in the 50's—racial discrimination was a major blight upon the history of our nation. I know well the bleak side of those days personally, as one who fought in the Civil Rights struggle and put the welfare of my own family on the line.

But generally in the 50's citizens knew safety in

our neighborhoods and streets. Children could play outside without fear. We didn't need to lock our cars just to run into the store. Basic trust among citizens allowed us to live with clearly-defined values. No one worried about high school riots and daily drug traffic. Most people agreed upon a lifestyle that was *right* and one that was *wrong.*

What happened? The Church abdicated its responsibility. The greatest error the Church ever committed was to stop addressing the needs of people and turn inward. Christians left the daily welfare of people in our society to agencies of the government. The Church split into two distinct factions, sometimes even within one denomination.

One side focused on people's spiritual well-being through evangelistically spreading the salvation message. The other group concentrated on feeding the poor and needy by focusing on fulfilling the social gospel. They hoped the Christian message would be welcomed eventually along with dependable, tangible provisions. Without both sides working and worshiping together, neither fulfilled their goals. God will never bless a divided Church by allowing them to have a powerful witness and lasting fruit. The Church gradually began losing the influence it once had in integrating biblical values into the moral fabric of our society.

A divided house will not stand. Humanists seized their chance. Education began to experience a flood of literature, history and science laced with *values clarification,* which emphasized that no one knew any clear answers for basic questions regarding the origin and purpose of life. The media ridiculed religion as being ignorant and superstitious. Political humanists slammed the doors on the Church's right to recognition in the public domain. Laws were passed not only forbidding public prayer, but also forbidding people's right to protest when speaking as Christians instead of speaking as citizens. The gap between Church and state, a gap never intended by our forefathers except to protect religious freedom, widened into a great chasm.

Sadly, most Christians didn't mind the opposition very much initially. They were happy doing their own things—planning Sunday School picnics, little devotionals for the teenagers, and Women's teas. Supporting missionaries in Africa and India soothed their conscience concerning outreach ministry. People's souls were the only concern—not their food and housing. Even concern for souls was selective. Many of these *evangelicals* never shared the gospel with someone of another race in their own hometown. Often white Christians seemed to be more concerned about the salvation of black Africans than black families living a mile away.

The black community organized to change their circumstances through demonstrations. The central force for change was found in black churches. The leaders stood behind pulpits on Sundays and marched in the streets during the week. Martin Luther King, Jr. was a man with a vision from God of unity and brotherhood. In spite of reported indiscretions which have attempted to mar his brilliant contribution to modern history, I firmly believe that Martin Luther King was a man chosen by God who followed a true spiritual vision. A movement which began as a vision from God became a political movement, and in my judgment, lost God's anointing upon it as a movement. But the dream of Martin Luther King is still very much alive today in racially-balanced congregations like my own in Atlanta.

Christians who aligned themselves with the social gospel became *do-gooders* who wondered why the poor increased in numbers and kept getting poorer. They seemed to be accomplishing very little in spite of their efforts. The government had more money, time and personnel to do the job of caring for people. Many social gospel Christians turned to politics, social action or civic groups. They wondered why there seemed to be so little power from God to accomplish their goals. Still they were critical of *hallelujah* Christians who were blind to the needs of hurting people around them. And their criticisms were justified in many respects.

Meanwhile, young people abandoned their parents' churches in great numbers because of religious superficiality and the irrelevance of the Church to the real world. Intellectualism replaced prayers in their problem-solving. No decade was more disillusioning than the sixties when the Baby Boomers began making major decisions in their lives: marriage partners, career choices and personal goals in life. I believe that the startling statistics today on family disintegration are the result of choices made by youth who had already lost all hope in making the world a better place.

The world was suddenly a very scary place in which to live. Assassinations. Vietnam. Eastern religions. Drugs. Watergate. Increase in crime. Increase in nuclear arms. Communist aggression. Political scandals. Runaway hippies. Flower Children. The anti-hero. Youth demanded answers for life, and they couldn't wait! Meanwhile, the Church rolled along in silence and isolation.

BREAKING THE SILENCE
WITH CLANGING CYMBALS

Probably nothing shook the humanistic political establishment more than the emergence of the *religious right*. Many aspects of the impact upon the political process of these conservative Christian activists have been positive—and many aspects have been terribly damaging to the primary mission of the Church.

The most positive aspect of the religious right is that some Christians finally spoke out in the political arena, breaking the almost total silence of a *moral majority* perceived to be weak and ineffective. Their most damaging contribution to Christianity involved stereotyping Christians in a conservative, evangelical mold at the expense of dedicated Christians whose social action would be perceived by the moral majority as liberal.

Conservative politics and Christianity may share many views in common, but they are not synonymous and never will be. I personally know politicians who are unquestionably Christians—both liberals and conservatives from both major political parties. I could name staunch conservatives who are not Christians at all. It's easy for the religious right to forget that people who belong to Jesus can think as liberals or conservatives, Republicans or Democrats, evangelicals or social gospel Christians. It's also easy for them to insist that conservatism represents Christian morality.

I prefer, like the Apostle Paul, to identify with every one of these groups for the sake of the gospel. All are found within my own congregation. The major political issues have far too many contingent factors to presume that all Christians are locked into one single opinion or are represented by one group politically. That view limits Christian influence across the board which should always be our goal.

The Bible must be our final authority in formulating opinions. Many issues concerning the right to life and quality living are clearly defined for Christians in Scripture. But biblical morality applied to modern society on other issues—capital punishment, the arms race, for example—are not so clearly interpreted. Hopefully, our opinions will come from reading Scripture, instead of searching for scriptures to support our opinions. Christians will never become carbon copies of one another in their total perceptions and political views, even within one church, much less within a nation.

We have an open forum at Chapel Hill Harvester Church for any political candidate to visit our congregation and greet the people. I do not endorse specific candidates running for office. I do address political issues—which are human issues—from a biblical perspective. I hope that I help my congregation to understand the importance of being informed on the issues and the candidates.

I certainly urge my congregation to vote prayerfully and intelligently in all primaries and general elections. In fact, we register voters in the foyer of our church on Sundays and Wednesday nights. Two of the presidential candidates, one from each major party, spoke from my pulpit on Sunday morning before the Super Tuesday primary in the southern states. I have met in a small group session with Vice-President George Bush.

Nevertheless, the Church must realize that its not the *might and power* of politicians or even the Christian community that is our hope. Great numbers of Christians are an asset to turning things around, but it will take much more than numbers. We need the direction of the Holy Spirit. We need Christian intercessors involved at the grass roots level. We need a clear definition of our purposes and goals in influencing government and secular society, and then boldness to do whatever God instructs us to do individually and corporately.

SECURING THE FUTURE

So what do we do? That's a good question! I was struck with an awesome realization at seeing the desire of Christians to do something at the *1988 Washington For Jesus* rally. People had driven thousands of miles, stood in cold rain and wind, prayed all day and marched around the Mall in front of the U.S. Capitol because they wanted *to do something* to turn our nation around before it is too late!

Christians sense the urgency of this hour! God will always honor such a willing response. But one designated day of prayer and spiritual demonstration is not enough. Prayer and responsible Christian action must be repeated every day for Christians to make a difference where they are across this nation. We've let things go too far and we've been silent too long. So how can we turn things around now?

First, learn how to release the Holy Spirit. "Binding the Strong Man," the Holy Spirit, can be the result of Christian apathy in the political process. We bind the Holy Spirit by believing that government, education, science or economics will solve our problems. God wants to use the hopelessness of our society to show Himself strong in our behalf. He is the source of solutions. The Holy Spirit is released first within us to our families, to our neighborhoods

197

and communities, to our cities and then, to our world. In a society that is in chaos, we must be bold in releasing the Holy Spirit.

Spiritual boldness may mean writing letters to congressmen and senators or to the editors of our local newspapers. Boldness may mean attending town hall meetings and letting other concerned citizens (as well as our legislators) know that Christians are convinced that the Church has solutions to community problems. We won't always be welcomed by everyone, but Christians will be surprised at how many citizens are waiting for someone of positive action to step forward with a plan, an idea or a possibility of solving their problems.

Learn to use the keys of the Kingdom. We must realize the power of binding evil forces and loosing the Holy Spirit over our circumstances, our cities and our nation. God is saying, "Let My Spirit go!" We must realize that Jesus gave His Church that authority as well as the mandate to use His authority, His name, on earth. Binding and loosing are called *keys* because they unlock the will of God to be realized on earth, and they lock spiritual wickedness from its effect on earthly circumstances.

Binding and loosing spirits allows spiritual authority in heaven to impact earth in a way that makes a difference. Jesus taught us to ask for God's will to come upon earth as it is in heaven. That only happens when we agree with God's will. We must also become channels in carrying out His will. We must both hear and do the things Jesus taught and did.

Learn to make intercession with Jesus Christ. The bride of Christ must agree with her Bridegroom. The call to intercession is upon the entire Church—

not just to a few Christians who have been called to a ministry of prayer. We become confident and empowered in intercession, in interaction with the Lord. The spiritual power we release to the world must first be released within our own hearts.

I am convinced that the Church wastes many prayers by asking for things which are not God's will at all. Effective intercession requires that we have the mind of Christ, His concerns, His burdens and His understanding of our needs. Where are the needs in the body of Christ today? This question could be answered in intercession over a local church, or intercession over a city or a nation.

I long for the day when within minutes the body of Christ will come into unity over some troubled place in the world where God has called for us to release His power through agreement. Of course, many Christians pray over the troubled spots on the evening news every day. But we can improve upon unity in activating our prayer power. I believe that modern technology is given for the benefit of proclaiming the gospel of the Kingdom around the globe and linking our intercession in singleness of mind and heart—as those in the upper room came into one mind and one accord on the Day of Pentecost (Acts 2:1,2). We need the wind of the Holy Spirit to blow fresh over Christians in China, Russia, Angola, Cuba.

The firstfruit of that dream has begun. Computer technology continues to link one ministry to another. We will soon have such a technological network in place that our spiritual network of intercession will be invincible against evil forces—if we use the tools God has given to us. Expect warfare in this area. The possibilities are tremendously threatening to satanic forces who understand the dangers of Christian unity and agreement with Jesus in intercession.

Learn to be a personal overcomer. The Bible calls Christians *overcomers* for a good reason. We are soldiers in a war. The battle rages. In a day when *things have gone too far* in losing our freedoms, and social corruption threatens the future of our children, we cannot afford the luxury of inaction. The trumpet has sounded for war! How do we fight? How do we win?

First, we must have *the blood of the Lamb* applied to our sins. Salvation is the foundational strategy of defeating Satan. We cannot save ourselves. Jesus Christ is our Savior, our Redeemer through the work of the cross. The power of grace through His atoning blood must become a reality to us in daily experience or we will always be too intimidated to engage in war against Satan.

Satan is an accuser who knows where to hit hardest. He'll kick us in weak areas; past failures, past hurts, loving relationships and the desires of our hearts. He'll dangle the carrot in front of our noses, and then jerk it away. But the grace of God is greater. The blood of Christ covers us and empowers us against any lies or accusations of the enemy. God delights in our overcoming faith against the wiles of the devil because Satan cannot understand self-denial, assurance in God's promises and endurance through the power of the Holy Spirit.

The second component of living as an overcomer is the *word of our testimony.* This strategy means boldness in our words. We speak God's will into the atmosphere. Life and death are in the power of the tongue. I have known Christians who kill the anointing of God's presence with negative reports and a lack of zeal and conviction in their testimonies. We need to understand the power of words, the creative force they become in the life of an overcomer.

Jesus spoke God's Word to the devil when He was tempted in the wilderness. In moments of temptation and feelings of defeat, we can also overcome the power of the enemy with God's Word, "It is written . . ." Once we understand the direction of God's will over our nation, we need to speak it forth boldly. God's Word admonishes us to say to the nations, "The Lord reigns" (Psalm 97:1). We are speaking that proclamation into the atmosphere—shaking the heavens, declaring a warning to forces of darkness that their time is running out.

Finally, we are overcomers through *loving not our lives unto death*. That attitude indicates an abandonment of self-will to the leading of the Holy Spirit. Such abandonment is supernatural, because our natural tendency is self-protection, self-will and self-satisfaction. Overcoming the devil means that we hold nothing back from Jesus as Lord of all areas of our lives—even if that means physical death as a witness for Him.

Jesus' description of the days before His coming indicates that Christians must be ready to face imprisonment, inquisitions and death sentences for the sake of the gospel (Matthew 24:8-10). The life of the Church at times has been quickened by the blood of martyrs. Jesus said that a seed falling to the ground yields much fruit. He goes on to speak one of the most profound paradoxes of Scripture, ". . . He who loves his life will lose it, and he who hates his life in this world will keep it for eternal life (John 12:25). Do Christians in the modern Church really believe these words of Jesus?

The Church in America could learn much from our brothers and sisters in Latin America in this hour. They do believe that overcoming means *loving not their lives unto death.* I have cried with many of these overcomers as they have spoken about the three-foot cells where they spent days of confinement under verbal abuse and mental torture. The mental torture is far worse than physical beatings which were also inflicted. One pastor heard the screams of a woman he was told was his wife. He *loved not his life unto death.* Soft, milquetoast Christianity will not survive in the days ahead. God is calling for overcomers in this critical hour! We need strong men and women who are willing to give their lives to the cause of Christ—regardless of the consequences.

Learn to move in a spirit of unity. The Church is a spiritual melting pot, a people who were not a people. We need many diverse pieces to complete the puzzle. Separate pieces fit together to form the total picture. The Bible describes us as members of one body. Do we believe and live that concept in the practice of Christian unity? Can we come into spiritual agreement on behalf of the survival of our families, our nation and our world.

God will not allow those opposing Christian unity to continue under His compassionate warning much longer. Too much is at stake. We need unity to become the witness God has called us to be to the ends of the earth—witnessing to every creature, discipling all nations. The power of agreement is so necessary to accomplish this mandate. Our agreement is not through intellectual assent or organizational structure or even great numbers of people, but through the unity of the Holy Spirit Who guides and directs our paths.

The eagle of the United States of America flutters his wings. His eyes are darkened. His feathers are scraggly and he moves with difficulty in pain. He was once a magnificent bird of strength and power— but he has been brutally attacked. Those given the responsibility of caring for him don't notice his wounds. They seem to be oblivious to his attackers while saying, "All is well. Let's relax. Let's amuse ourselves. It's such a beautiful day to eat, drink and be merry."

But some see the signs of warning, hear the cries of pain and realize the urgency of this hour to pray, to join together, to act in faith under the Holy Spirit's direction. God is saying, "Choose this day whom you will serve." That choice is costly. We can serve ourselves today and pay later with the loss of freedom in the lives of our children, or we can pay the price of obedience today and live eternally as a generation of God's people who heard His voice and acted in obedience to Him. The choice is made individually and enacted corporately. I have decided. As for me and my house, we will serve the Lord!

Chapter Eight
Spiritual Trends

† The further society strays from biblical values, the more absurd Christians' lifestyles will seem in contrast to social expectations.

† The media will continue to promote an atmosphere of fear and instability for society.

† The Church will begin to understand the role of the Holy Spirit as comforter in maintaining a sound mind in daily living.

† Deceptive religions, such as the New Age Movement, will flourish in these days because people are growing spiritually hungry in a society with such unstable values.

† The Church will begin to understand the threat sinful thoughts pose to the morality of their environment.

† The Church will be forced to "have the mind of Christ" in order to survive in a corrupt society.

† Increasingly, people advocating a worldly view of life as *normal* will attempt to discredit the mental stability of people who are dedicated to the cause of God.

† The counsel of eldership in the body of Christ must begin to discern the precise direction which God will give His Church in these days to accomplish His purposes.

† Some people will take actions under the guise of *spiritual direction* which will bring the Church into persecution.

† Motivations in ministry will be tested through discipline.

† Pseudo-Christianity, which breeds mental confusion, will be built on a foundation of fulfilling personal desires.

† Christians who minister out of a sense of duty to God will fall into deception.

† Deceived Christians will believe it is their duty to purge the Church of sin and error.
† Christian discipline will follow a decision for Christ, and will become a powerful witness to others.
† Christians will realize that fulfilling their destinies to be like Christ brings true fulfillment.
† Obedience to Christ limits human choice, and Christians will begin to discover the meaning of walking a *narrow way.*
† Satanic attacks on Christians' minds begin with what they think of themselves, then others, then God.
† Medical breakthroughs will come as a result of probing the relationship between the processes of the mind and the body.
† A sound mind will be deliberately cultivated and protected.
† God will give ministers insight on dealing with depression in their lives and the lives of those for whom they are responsible.
† The Church's identity will be the key to mental health.
† Greater attacks than ever before will occur in the minds of Christians in the days ahead.

8

MENTALLY ALERT TO FACE TOMORROW

In a world gone crazy, normal seems absurd. We live in a world where the kids who haven't tried marijuana, cigarettes or alcoholic beverages by the time they graduate from high school are thought to be peculiar. Teenage girls and boys who save themselves for marriage are considered to be deprived. Men who turn down the fast dollar because they won't walk on someone else to get ahead are said to have no ambition. Women who don't push their husbands and children to form relationships with people who are useful to them for a social boost are called uncaring.

Meanwhile, our mental computers are storing input. Soap operas set the standards for social morality. Late night television humor is mocking and profane. Rock music videos flood our *family rooms* with surrealistic, bizarre scenes loaded with sexual innuendos and demonic symbolism as art. Magazines tell us to shape up, dress better, lose weight, spend more, go further, be smarter and make it happen! Go! Go! Go! Push! Push! Push! Advertisers tell us to buy their products to make all our dreams come true.

Even our news does not give us much information. Editorial comments criticizing our country's leaders, the latest international controversy, crimes of the day, updates on recent scandals and off-beat stories capture our attention and make our lives seem dull by comparison.

Our thinking is so jaded that only negative news is interesting. A story of hope becomes a token story at the end of the broadcast, insignificantly entertaining. News is followed by three hours of prime time detectives chasing murderers, sordid love affairs in irreconcilable alliances, or offbeat characters in situation comedies. Then we wonder why people live in fear; why we ask ourselves the ominous question, "What is wrong with me?"

Did Jesus see our confused generation when He promised to send us a Comforter? Can the Holy Spirit's comfort cover our minds for daily living as well as embrace us during those especially stressful times like the death of a loved one? Let's look closely at the spiritually-minded Christian living in a perverse generation. How can he survive the pressure? How does a Christian maintain a sound mind in a mad, mad world?

Is it any wonder that millions of dollars are spent each year to maintain the sanity of people who are facing mental stress? Pills to induce sleep or to give people energy, shock treatments, psychological counseling, medication for chemical imbalances, tranquilizers, painkillers, etc., are all intended to help us maintain sanity. Thousands of people are institutionalized for mental disorders every year. Almost everyone needs counseling at some time to face a crisis, overcome periods of depression or handle overwhelming stress.

Conditions in a mad, mad world drive most people at some point to seek refuge in religion. For many of these truth-seekers, their spiritual quests prove to be disappointing ventures that cause them to abandon *religion* altogether. For example, the surge in growth among those joining the New Age Movement is an indication of spiritual hunger among people living in a mad, mad world. I tremble at the implications of thousands of people under the power of the occult.

The New Age is an *anything goes* religion that teaches the *ancient art* of mystical channeling and crystals producing a *harmonic convergence* in *fields of energy*. Reincarnation, meditation and extrasensory perception are all New Age trappings. New Age faith healers are able to *read auras*. It has become a fad to some and a way of life to others. Actress Shirley MacLaine is perhaps the most famous advocate, promoting New Age practices in books and personal appearances on television talk shows and lectures.

The New Age Movement is growing. According to a feature article in *Time Magazine:*

Bantam Books says its New Age titles have increased tenfold in the past decade. The number of New Age bookstores has doubled in the past five years to about 2,500. New Age radio is spreading with . . . light jazz that one listener described as "like I tapped into a radio station on

Mars." The Grammys now include a special award for New Age music. Fledgling magazines with names like *New Age, Body Mind Spirit,* and *Brain/Mind Bulletin* are full of odd adds, *Healing yourself with crystals, American Indian magic can work for you, How to use a green candle to gain money, The power of the pendulum can be in your hands, Use numerology to win the lottery.* And perhaps inevitably, *New health through colon rejuvenation.*

Time Magazine, December, 1987, p.62.

Is religion merely "an opiate of the masses," as Karl Marx argued? A mental game of survival? Mind over matter? Positive or negative chemical vibrations in the brain? Does it really matter which religion a person plugs into? Is Christian faith no more than a mental reprieve from life's harsh realities? Or is faith a viable means of confronting and overcoming obstacles in life through choosing eternal values for eternal purposes?

THE BATTLEFIELD

Christian teachers warn that the mind is the battlefield of the soul and the spirit. Satanic oppression upon the mind is as much a reality as the world we see and touch. Jesus made some very interesting comments on Judaic law (the Ten Commandments) by expanding the commonly-accepted definition of sin as actions against God to the realm of one's thought life.

Jesus said that lust is the same spiritual sin as adultery; hate is the same as murder (Matthew 5:21-28). In other words, a very moral person who harbors evil thoughts can be as sinful against God in spirit as one who breaks moral laws with his actions. No wonder such teaching provoked religious leaders in Jesus' day and continues to do so today, stimulating challenges and discussions. Even true, born-again Christians accept the concept—only because Jesus said it. Human beings are far more hard-nosed toward sinful actions than thoughts. Sinful actions have unhappy consequences to other people, while sinful thoughts spare others in most ways. It is inevitable, of course, that one harboring evil thoughts will eventually produce evil actions, "For as he thinks in his heart, so is he . . ." (Proverbs 23:7).

One undeniable fact emerges from all of Jesus' teaching: the inner world of our minds is very important to God. Sinful thoughts need to be surfaced, confessed and forgiven, so that our minds can be renewed. As incredible as it sounds, Scripture teaches that a Christian can have the "mind of Christ" (1 Corinthians 2:16). We must also realize quickly that the "mind of Christ" conflicts with the mind of this world (Romans 12:2).

Society's moral standards are in constant evolution. Changing morals reflect society's changing attitudes toward acceptable behavior in any period of history. Changing standards of acceptable behavior create difficulty in coping with life for everyone in one way or another. These changes produce the generation gap, for example. An older generation works with a different frame of reference of social morality than a younger generation.

Let me add quickly that God's view of righteousness is unchanging. Biblical laws are absolute laws governing human nature, whether they are acknowledged by the majority of people in society or not. A society that has strayed far off course from God's purposes for creation will inevitably turn on those who hold to God's standards. The *gap* between society and Christians' lifestyles is too wide to make them acceptable.

Increasingly in our day, people advocating a worldly view of life as *normal* will attempt to discredit people who are dedicated to the cause of God. One of the most frequent attacks of secular society against a bold Christian focuses on calling a Christian's mental stability into question. Belief in God is perceived to be a crutch, a sign of weakness.

For example, any evaluations of spiritual direction made by the secular press make spiritual men and women sound totally ridiculous. A magazine article will discuss a certain ministry's direction in the same objective tone as they discuss the stock market trading. No one can read the events recorded in Scripture without agreeing that actions in obedience to God contradict a society's codes and standards. This is especially true in a wicked and perverse generation.

The more corrupt the moral standards of a nation become, the more God's standards of righteousness conflict with the norms of that society. I am not referring to great exploits of faith, I am referring to people living out basic biblical morality. And fueling the fire even more, many of the leading patriarchs of the Bible—prophets like Jeremiah, Ezekiel and John the Baptist—exhibited at times what would be considered extreme actions, though they moved in total obedience to God's voice.

Numerous acts of faith recorded in the Bible—Noah's building the ark, Abraham's willingness to sacrifice Isaac on an altar, Israel's seven days of marching around the walls of Jericho, David's seemingly inhumane conquest of cities in bloody wars, Jesus' using a whip to drive out moneychangers from the temple—would cause any objective observer to question the sanity of the one displaying such actions.

I must warn that discernment among eldership is always necessary in evaluating extreme behavior as being God's will. Christians must never resort to *pseudo-spirituality* to justify any actions they take under the guise of *spiritual direction.* Godly men and women who take actions which would be categorized as extreme must be certain they are hearing Jesus' voice; that their actions conform to the image and character of Christ recorded in Scripture, and that they stand submitted to the discerning scrutiny of elders in the body of Christ. Numerous atrocities have been committed in the name of God. Scriptures clearly state that these historical blights on Christianity were never ordained according to God's purposes for mankind.

For both Christians and non-Christians, no aspect of facing the future is more threatening than mental instability. People under pressure realize they are near a breaking point. Numerous diseases affecting the mind, such as Alzheimer's disease and society's general acceptance of senility as a symptom of old age, call into question the validity of claiming God's promises of abundant living as a life-long expectation.

Everyone wants to be mentally healthy. No factor of quality living is more central to every other issue of life than maintaining a sound mind. Financial prosperity, accomplishments, talents and opportunities are all wasted when one becomes mentally distraught. The threat of mental illness affects everyone regardless of social, educational, racial or economic status. The same circumstantial pressures causing one person to emerge heroic and strong may break the confidence of someone else, plunging them into deep depression or irrational actions. Why?

Conditions of *the mind* clearly relate to one's heredity, environmental nurturing from experiences beginning in the early years of life, and both innate and cultivated spiritual sensitivity. A study of human behavior involves examining numerous factors that determine one's capacity for enjoying mental health for a lifetime. However, God has given specific answers concerning maintaining mental health regardless of hereditary or environmental factors.

God's Word provides precepts to set one's course toward maintaining a sound mind and balancing spiritual and natural expectations within one's social environment. God is calling His Church to maturity. He is calling His Church to demonstrate the spiritual reality of their position in the heavens within the tangible realities of their daily lives on earth. This is one meaning of Jesus' prayer, ". . . Your Kingdom come . . . on earth as it is in heaven . . ." (Luke 11:2).

Because the mind is the primary battlefield of satanic warfare, I believe that mental preparation for the inevitable social stresses of the future is essential. A chaotic society labels true wisdom as being *insanity*. Spiritual truth conflicts with carnal social perspectives. In days of widespread deception, the importance of having a sound mind and having the ability to discern the mental stability of others according to the standards of God's Word provides safety and sure spiritual direction.

We can be certain that a sound mind is God's will for us. Part of our armor for spiritual warfare is *the helmet of salvation* which covers our minds. The Holy Spirit is not the author of confusion. A Christian who demonstrates a Kingdom witness will exemplify righteousness, peace and joy in his countenance, attitude, words and behavior.

One who has a sound mind will also be a channel for bringing the peace of God to others, even to people in the throes of turbulent circumstances. A person who has a sound mind is one who engenders the trust of others in the decisions he makes. He is able to offer stability and direction according to God's Word in any circumstance. For that reason, a sound mind is essential for a Christian to lead others into spiritual truth and to minister to their needs.

OBSTACLES TO MENTAL HEALTH

What are some of the obstacles to enjoying a sound mind? Too often I have watched Christians begin to move in obedience to the Holy Spirit's direction and then stray off track. At times of openness in prayer or under spiritual conviction, people often make promises to God that they cannot fulfill. Guilt and fear flood the mind when we realize an inability to follow through on vows spoken to God.

Spiritual failure torments our minds. We lose confidence before God and numerous problems spring up in our lives as a result. We feel unworthy. We reject God's will because we believe it to be too difficult, therefore we feel rejected by God, then by others as well. We turn away from our very source of help when we avoid the outstretched arms of a loving, merciful Father Who wants to restore us. He says, ". . . Come to Me . . . I will give you rest" (Matthew 11:28).

I am convinced that the spiritual motivation of one's heart makes all the difference in maintaining a sound mind. Our motivation is always tested in discipline. A sound mind is a disciplined mind. Spiritual discipline is impossible to maintain when one pursues self-serving goals rather than seeks to please God first. Until one learns to discipline the flesh in his thoughts and actions, he never learns the discipline of the Spirit.

Before addressing other principles of maintaining

a sound mind, allow me to warn Christians of a treacherous path too many take, believing they are following God's will. This path will never produce the sound mind of a spiritually mature Christian. This path always leads to failure, frustration and even spiritual disillusionment. Many people with genuine callings from God upon their lives have left the ministry because they have walked this path.

Immature Christians who are mentally confused focus on *personal desires*. Initially, our desires are neither good nor evil. Only keen discernment can help us foresee the dangers of our desires in the early stages. In fact, our desires may appear to be very noble and spiritual. Even fleshly desires indicate mental health when they remain under the control of the Holy Spirit.

Our desires become destructive when they serve as the foundation of our spiritual commitment. Perhaps we claim the fulfillment of our desires according to scriptural promises such as "Delight yourself also in the Lord, and He shall give you the desires of your heart" (Psalm 37:4). We justify seeking to fulfill those desires by defining them as being our rights according to God's Word.

Our desires are like a door. That door may open to a life spent gratifying pride or ego, or it may eventually open us to a deep commitment to the cause of Christ. Though desires seem to be rather neutral in their early stages, they quickly become positive or negative forces in our lives. Inevitably, when we maintain spiritual discipline based solely upon our personal desires, those desires for Christian service become a sense of duty.

Duty is a feeling of obligation. Duty implies servitude or slavery. Jesus clearly indicated that people serve only one master. A person who is duty-bound serves his obligations as if they were a master ruling over him. Overly ambitious people stand as clear examples of those bound to their duties in order to satisfy their desires.

Ambition serves a self-centered ego. Many times in conversations with *ambitious people,* we realize that their desires are demanding masters that force them to serve their egos. They focus on their duties as top priorities—not to serve God (though they may seem to be working for the Kingdom)—but to serve themselves.

Some people serve relationships. Everything they do serves a relationship as if they were servants bound to strict duties in order to maintain that relationship. Any threats to that relationship drive them to despair. They obviously do not trust God with that person to whom they are obsessively committed. Such relationships may appear to others to be spiritually wholesome and born of God. In truth, duty dictates apparent *emotional caring* so much that the relationship becomes a destructive barrier to the true potential of God's will in their lives.

When giving to God and serving God become duties, a Christian's mental health is in trouble. Paul said, ". . . not of necessity . . ." in regard to responding to God's will. Duty-bound Christian service is of no benefit to the Kingdom of God. This service offers no spiritual life to share with others. Such service lacks thanksgiving to God for the opportunities to serve Him. Duty-bound Christians feel pressured by demands and heavy burdens. They lose that sense of fulfillment that accompanies love for God and for His people. Inevitably, duty leads a Christian along a destructive path away from a sound mind. Duty leads to spiritual deception.

Desires, which become duties, draw people into *deception.* The Bible says that "There is a way which seems right to a man, but its end is the way of death . . ." (Proverbs 14:12). Deceived people are religious and sincere, but their controlling egos dictate to them, "I need recognition! Look what I have done! Everyone should appreciate my calling and my talent!"

Destruction overtakes deceived people. They usually blame others for their own failure in achieving the fulfillment of their desires. When spiritual leaders see the danger signals and attempt to correct them, they will likely react with hostility. They reason to themselves that this authority figure in their lives must be jealous of them, or fails to recognize the value of their talent to the ministry. People in deception are always defensive and easily offended.

A deceived person is convinced that the Word of God supports his case. He has an *I'm doing God a favor* attitude. One of the most blatant examples of deception in the Church today is the work of people who believe that they are called *to purify* the Church. We have seen this deception manifested in top positions of major ministries who have recently fallen. They publicly stated judgments against others in the ministry and now they are being judged themselves by their own standards.

A person involved in deception could be a secretary, a children's worker, a choir member or someone working in another department of the church in a supporting role. He assumes responsibility for purging the ministries of people around him, a responsibility that belongs to the work of the Holy Spirit alone. He prays, "God, help me to straighten out this mess!" His accusations of others are justified in his own mind as being God's will. That assumption is deception in its most destructive form.

Persecutors begin with seemingly pure desires to

see the Church purged of sin and error. Deception begins when all they can see is the *speck* in other people's eyes. Once they begin focusing their attention (and teaching) on the wrongs of other Christians, they become duty-bound to defend their perspective. They become pressured by their audiences to take actions against those whom they criticize.

When desires for holiness create a negative attitude instead of a loving attitude toward restoring others, one's duty to take action forces him into further deception. Christians' lives are destroyed. The body of Christ is wounded. What is the scriptural basis for such actions? Under whose authority is such destruction unleashed? Deceived people become *laws unto themselves*. Correction only comes by true repentance before God—a repentance of heart and spirit, not of words alone.

Now I'll discuss the path leading Christians toward maintaining a sound mind in a mad, mad world. Once again, we must probe the foundational motivations of the heart. Instead of desire, the foundation of a sound mind is a decision to follow Christ at any cost. Decision is the first step—then desires follow as the fruit of that decision.

Decisions must be made in accordance with the teachings of Scripture. God is a God of covenant. He takes our vows very seriously. "He who swears to his own hurt . . ." means that a decision stands even when the pain of that decision becomes a reality we must somehow endure (Psalm 15:4). Of course, assurance that a decision will be tested by God motivates us to make wise decisions. Decisions of the flesh cannot be maintained under the fires of testing. Decisions of the Spirit will stand. Foolish decisions break our confidence before God and hinder our witness to the world.

A decision becomes the trigger for our actions. Choices in our lives begin to conform to the direction of our decisions. Following a decision, we develop the necessary discipline to confirm that decision in our everyday experiences. Perhaps others will play significant roles in allowing the decisions we have made before God to become reality. We even need to protect our decisions whenever Satan tries to rob us of a commitment we have made to follow God's will.

Spiritual *discipline* means denying ourselves, taking up a cross and following Christ. Discipline cannot be separated from one's purpose in life. Following Jesus' example is a deliberate, life-long course of action which constantly tests our motivations and purposes. Too many Christians make glib promises to God that last only a few hours or days. The level of one's commitment to his decisions before God will determine his commitment to discipline his thoughts, desires and actions.

Any desires which contradict one's original decision in following Christ must be quickly discarded. Our desires should conform to the obedience of Christ. This is the place where so many Christians lose sight of God's perfect plan for their lives. They discount their decisions whenever their desires begin to pull them in another direction. Suddenly all of their mental processes focus on fulfilling their desires. The most effective strategy to combat this is to declare a decision for Christ openly as soon as it is made and continue to confirm it with your words. Don't hesitate to verbalize your decision!

I was studying to become a civil engineer and was the president of the sophomore class at Furman University when God called me into the ministry. Immediately, I told everyone that I had been called to preach and went directly to the counselors' offices to change my course of study. I knew that unless I told everyone immediately, that decision would be impossible for me to maintain. Social pressures and ambition would have trapped me into a compromise.

By declaring my decision to follow God's will for my life, I opened my heart for God to build protection around me that enabled me to walk the path of the decision to follow His will. Yes, my decision continued to be tested in my relationships, finances, academics, emotions, etc. But through the testing, my proclamation of God's purposes for my life was essential in enabling me to fulfill my commitment to the Lord. That declaration was like a stake driven into the ground.

The ultimate end of our decisions and discipline is the likeness of Christ within us; to have "the mind of Christ." Fulfilling our *destiny* through Jesus Christ is the only true fulfillment that life has to offer. Any other achievement is temporal success, a counterfeit of true joy.

Confrontations and battles over one's destiny in Christ are inevitable. For twelve years my family and I followed a vision from God for a worldwide ministry while pastoring a small, struggling congregation in Atlanta's inner city. We had absolutely no evidence that the vision God had given to me was ever possible— but I had made a decision to discipline my life in the direction of my calling from the Lord. Once God had allowed that decision to be tested and the discipline to be proven, the vision began to unfold quickly into reality. I was as amazed as anyone else at how God worked out His plan!

How committed are we to our decisions to give our lives to Christ? Will our decisions stand the tests of criticism, scorn and adverse circumstances? Will we maintain a sound mind when others around us are falling apart emotionally and urging us to compromise or quit? Are we willing to give God the glory when our decisions begin to be realized?

Jesus made a decision during that night of agonizing prayer in the Garden of Gethsemane. Every word and movement in those final hours following His encounter with God concerning His destiny were totally governed by the decision He made in the Garden. Once He yielded His will to the Father, He never wavered in moving according to that decision.

Jesus' decision went against His fleshly desires, His own will and His own plan. What an example for us! No wonder the leading of the Holy Spirit is often not the way that *seems right* to us! A decision in obedience to Christ always limits human choices. Therefore, few Christians really understand this spiritual law. We sing about *the narrow way* without fully comprehending the reality of walking the narrow path. Christians who do walk it will usually seem to be extreme in their dedication. In truth, they understand the power of self-denial.

How do we spiritually prepare for satanic attacks upon our minds? The first area of attack will probably focus on what we think about ourselves. Insane people believe that they are gods or queens or famous historical personalities. They have lost all personal identity in the ability to see the realities of life.

Satanic forces will probably attempt to get a Christian to regard himself as being more special, valuable, talented, etc., than others. Vanity is an open door for mental problems. Expectations are out of reach. We always compare ourselves with others to feel justified in our feelings. Someone must be blamed for being an obstacle in the way of realizing our goals. Satanic oppression makes us want to blame someone other than ourselves. Ambition and stress-related problems can lead to mental instability.

Secondly, mental warfare involves how we relate to other people. One of the first signs of insanity is withdrawal from a group. Imposed isolation is one of the first indications of an emotional problem. Perhaps withdrawal indicates oppression from spirits of rejection, neglect, or some other emotional pain we have battled since childhood. Spirits of infirmity may isolate people and cause them to draw back from others like a wounded animal. Negative feelings often cause sicknesses. Real physical ailments result, but the root of the physical problems is mental oppression.

People are often withdrawing from God when they back away from members of the body of Christ. Scripture teaches that we cannot love an invisible God and then fail to love God's visible people, but mentally oppressed Christians are often unable to practice that teaching. When those feelings of withdrawal begin to surface within us, we need to sort through our feelings to find problem areas which open doors to satanic oppression upon our minds. A steady diet of God's Word can help to shed light upon these problem areas and confront the negative thought processes that gain control of our thinking.

The Bible says to "comfort the feebleminded," (I Thessalonians 5:14 OKJ) and many people believe that this verse refers to people who are mentally ill. The meaning of this verse actually refers to those who do not have a strong will, people who lack spiritual fortitude. Many people die prematurely because they lack the will to fight to the end of their course.

Comforting feebleminded people probably means to *stir them up*. Encouragement, exhortation and building confidence in someone is a way to stir up the will of God within them—and that is certainly the role of the supreme Comforter (the Holy Spirit) in every Christian's life. Should we not follow His example in comforting one another by stirring up faith?

Some of the saddest people on earth are those who have a retirement mentality and are waiting to die. I am so opposed to the commonly accepted social concept of retirement. Visit a rest home and discern the spirit over it. How much we need Kingdom creativity in solving this social injustice! Retirement is an injustice to human dignity. Scripture gives no basis for putting away people whom society decides are no longer functioning at full physical/mental capacity due to the processes of aging.

We commit such an injustice to insist upon people's retirement based upon their chronological age. The Bible says of Moses that until the time of his death ". . . His eyes were not dim nor his natural vigor abated" (Deuteronomy 34:7). Scripture only indicates that we can expect to enjoy mental health throughout life.

Of course, the physical, chemical changes in the body do affect one's mental health at various stages in life. Menopause is a physical change that usually causes periods of mental anxiety and emotional trauma as the body adjusts chemically to ending the physical ability to produce children.

When the chemistry of our physical bodies changes, we naturally feel new emotions. The *hot flashes* of menopause become a physical reaction that generates an emotional response in women's minds. Fainting is a frightening experience of losing control that relates directly to physical and mental pressures. Startling news—especially if it concerns people we love—causes a physical response to a mental trauma.

Expect some breakthroughs in medicine as the mysteries between the processes of the mind affecting resistance to disease and physical health begin to unfold. Stress makes one prone to sickness. The glands of the body react quickly to danger signals from our minds. One who has a sound mind does not allow physical reactions to dominate his thinking processes. We either react or respond to physical and emotional signals to our brains. Crisis situations always test the soundness of our minds.

As a pastor counseling people for over forty years, I can attest to the fact that both men and women go through menopause. Physical adjustments during menopause for women are more obvious, of course, but men suffer the same emotional fears. Like women who face the trauma of no longer being able to bear children, men are also convinced that they are no longer needed, life's achievements are ending, and they are losing sexual attractiveness. These feelings can follow so many destructive paths. Such feelings harbored over a period of time can cause a state of deep depression.

Depression's root causes are feelings of inadequacy and lack of self-esteem. Depressed people do not believe that they can function at an acceptable level of performance. They back away from any situation that puts them under demands, stress or the evaluations of others. Depression at any stage of life is related far less to age than to coping with life's demands. I've counseled numerous men and women between the ages of twenty-five and thirty-five who are gripped by depression. Stress has robbed them of their ability to cope adequately with the pressures they must face. Nature puts their minds *on hold* in a state of depression until they can feel worthy again.

"God has not given us a spirit of fear, but of power and of love and of a sound mind" (2 Timothy 1:7). Fear is the basic cause of mental illness: fear of failure, fear of old age, fear of losing attractiveness, fear of losing relationships, fear of God's judgment. All these fears rob us of the abundant life which Jesus assured us He came to provide. The antidote for fear is found in this same verse: God has given us power, love and a sound mind.

I experienced a time of depression when I was about twenty-seven years old. I had assumed the pastorate of a large church in Atlanta, a job too great for me to have felt any sense of adequacy in handling the complex problems I faced. But God knows how I tried! Instead of coping, I felt repeated failure. I found myself in the depths of depression. At an age when a man should be at his most healthy productivity, I was totally out-of-balance and ready to give up.

I felt that I needed to prove to the elders of the church that I was capable of being their pastor. I felt guilty for any time spent on anything other than ministry. I knew that prayer was my only hope, so I set my alarm for four o'clock each morning to pray. That discipline carried me though the period of stress and probably prevented my experiencing a total mental collapse.

Communion with God also enabled me to continue loving people. God had granted me the gift of love for His people while I was still a student in seminary. During the most trying time in my life, fighting for my sanity, I still felt the intensity of God's love within me toward the people I served. The discipline of prayer and the power of love brought me through that depression. That discipline literally saved my life.

A sound mind must be deliberately cultivated and protected. No one can maintain a sound mind without discipline because oppressive forces war against any channel of God's power and love. The battles over the mind are greatest for those who are most yielded to God's will. Obedient Christians threaten the powers of darkness.

Most people will never admit to the mental battles they fight—especially if they are Christian leaders. All of us fight to maintain a sound mind. Neurotic behavior often takes the form of ridiculous games that perfectly rational people play within their minds. People walk around an object a certain way; they enter into mental debate over insignificant matters; they talk to themselves; they pretend to be someone else. Everyone is somewhat neurotic at times. Right? Be honest!

Mentally healthy people are able to admit whenever they need help in some area of emotional or spiritual conflict. Healthy people want to live, relate to others and accomplish the decisions they have made to serve God. Depression throws healthy desires in reverse. Depressed people respond to life with irrational actions. Years ago I counseled a young man who walked the halls of his high school with his hands held high in the air. He told me that an inner voice instructed him to praise the Lord as he walked to classes. As I began to probe deeper into that young man's perspective on life, I discovered a behavior problem covering deep depression.

I went to visit a young wife and mother who had been physically ill. As her husband opened the door into their bedroom, she said to me, "Be careful, Pastor. You are entering the belly of the whale." The woman's words were not spoken as poetic metaphor—she had lost touch with reality.

The worst way I could have responded to this woman would have been to say, "Snap out of it!" That command not only would have been impossible for her, it would have driven her behind silent walls to hide her thoughts from anyone. The more that people in mental distress open themselves to someone else, the more likely they are to get well. People with mental problems cannot help themselves. Communication means survival, and they need love from others. We must allow them time to cope with the jumble of thoughts and feelings which make them feel numb inside.

Spiritual oppression is satanic and leads to depression, neurotic behavior and sometimes even psychotic behavior. Oppression comes to us as a spirit— sometimes through a spirit operating in another person. People who have lived together for a number of years actually can take on each other's spirits. They look alike, sound alike and share the same physical, emotional and mental problems.

Some may think this is a strange observation, but even animals can carry spirits that oppress people. Extreme attachments to animals can be quite threatening to one's mental health. I hope animal lovers won't attack me for that statement! I know that caring for animals can also be therapeutic, but some animals' personalities are extremely controlling. We need to be aware of our emotional attachments in all areas of our lives because our affections directly influence our mental stability and spiritual growth.

The book of Daniel tells the story of King Nebuchadnezzar who went insane. The cause of the king's madness was a failure to recognize God's authority:

This is the interpretation, O king, and this is the decree of the Most High, which has come upon my lord the king: They shall drive you from men, your dwelling shall be with the beasts of the field, and they shal@ make you eat grass like oxen. They shall wet you with the dew of heaven, and seven times shall pass over you, till you know that the Most High rules in the kingdom of men, and gives it to whomever He chooses. (Daniel 4:24,25)

Knowing God and who we are in relation to Him gives us proper identity. Identity is the key to having a sound mind. God exalts and abases a person according to that person's response to Him. We must understand that in spite of the chaotic conditions of our world, God is the final authority within the kingdom of men. Learning to accept our station and position in the kingdom of men as well as the Kingdom of God is evidence of sanity. Trying to be someone other than the person God created us to be will put us under insurmountable pressures and destroy our minds.

People often ask me how I survive the schedule I keep between preaching, counseling, church administration, outreach ministry and traveling. My only answer is that I'm called to do what I am doing. I would never ask another person to attempt to keep my schedule—I would advise them to slow down!

Anyone who assumes pressures of life outside his calling from God is on his way to mental collapse. In fact, the statistics on mental breakdowns among men and women in ministry are staggering and continually rising. Why? Many people minister at levels of responsibility to which they were never called.

Mental survival is impossible beyond one's calling. Weariness and frustration overpower a man who is ministering beyond his spiritual preparation and maturity. Moral problems and emotional problems in that minister's life result—leaving trusting people who followed his direction in absolute devastation. I could give numerous examples of this situation. A person's finding his proper place in God's will allows him to cope with any struggles or challenges that come.

Jesus delivered a man from a legion of demonic spirits which had driven the man insane (Mark 5:1-20). How did the man's demonic possession begin? Perhaps he had feelings of inadequacy, rejection or even pride which opened the door to spirits controlling his thoughts. The man roamed the tombs, crying out, cutting himself with stones. After Jesus delivered him, Jesus insisted that the man return to his family. People who follow ministries from town to town are not demonstrating spiritual wholeness and maturity—they are babes. Christians who put Kingdom principles to work at home are God's true witnesses.

So the first principle in maintaining a sound mind is learning to control our thought processes. Once again, discipline is imperative. A vain imagination, wishful thinking, fantasizing, neurotic behavior patterns which become habits, all open our thoughts to mental oppression. We must boldly confront our thought processes, even saying to ourselves, "I will not allow my mind to go in that direction!" The Bible promises that mental control is possible.

Regardless of the pressures or the enemy's attacks, we have the power to control our thoughts. Forgetfulness due to age is no excuse. People forget details they do not want to remember—then look for excuses. Our minds work in a way similar to a muscle in the body. Lack of exercise begins muscular atrophy. How do we avoid spiritual atrophy? Getting up early in the morning to enjoy fellowship with God in prayer and in His Word sets a person on a path toward maintaining mental health for that day. We absolutely must exercise discipline in our thoughts and actions. We give God control of our thoughts by resisting the comforts of a warm bed to spend time with Him.

Secondly, we maintain a sound mind when we think on good things. God's Word is very specific in His instructions on the content of our thoughts. God even presses us to reject some thoughts—malice, hypocrisy, envy—and to dwell on good thoughts which are true, noble, pure, lovely, virtuous and praiseworthy (1 Peter 2:1; Philippians 4:8). Good thoughts ensure peace.

How seldom we realize that controlling our thoughts becomes a matter of obedience or disobedience to God. Too often, we're convinced we have a right to worry. We even read newspapers and magazines featuring negative *facts* that fill our minds with evil details. As I have stated, television news focuses on negative reports that flood our homes with ungodly thinking under the guise of keeping us well-informed. I am not suggesting that Christians should not watch television news or read newspapers. I am advocating that Christians realize that we live in an unwholesome social environment that breeds doubt, suspicion, fear and moral instability. Our witness of the Kingdom of God offers society its only hope, but we must influence society—not allow society to dominate our thinking.

> Finally, brethren, whatever things are true, whatever things are noble, whatever things are just, whatever things are pure, whatever things are lovely, whatever things are of good report, if there is any virtue and if there is anything praiseworthy—meditate on these things. The things which you learned and received and heard and saw in me, these do, and the God of peace will be with you. (Philippians 4:8,9)

When someone who is locked in the grips of depression comes to me for counseling, often I take a hat or an empty vase and ask them what they see inside. They reply, "It's empty." Then I take objects off my desk—pencils, letters, paper clips—and put them inside the container. I ask them again what is inside. They name the objects. I take those objects out and fill the container with mints. "What's inside now?" They answer, "Mints." Then I say to them, "Your mind is like this container. If you fill your mind with anxiety, criticism, bitterness and comparisons with others, you'll be mentally sick. If you fill your mind with good things, you'll begin to realize that life is worthwhile."

We must remember how to laugh. People who can bring laughter to our lives are gifts from God—though they often don't realize how spiritually gifted they are! Two of my associate pastors enjoy laughing so much that it's almost dangerous for them to sit side by side in a Sunday service. Something humorous occurs and those two are totally gone! I try to look at them like an austere father, but it's usually too late! We enjoy laughter at Chapel Hill Harvester Church. I think God enjoys laughing with us, too!

Sometimes we have to look high and low for good things to meditate upon, but the effort is well worth it. When the meditations of our hearts please God, we have confidence—no matter what situation we are facing. The Bible also refers to lustful, lewd minds in the last days that are totally out of control. What a contrast!

I know I run a risk in writing this, but ministers who constantly rail against choreographed dancing and dangerous women often fight moral battles on a personal level. Note the content of sermons in the days ahead. Are they pure and peaceable? Do they exhort people toward thinking good, noble thoughts—or constantly warn them against lustful thoughts? Everyone knows that lust is not pleasing to God! An emphasis on these matters surfaces problems within the preacher. "To the pure all things are pure . . ." (Titus 1:15).

Thirdly, we maintain a sound mind with power from God. Power comes in prayer, a consistent study of God's Word and fellowship in the body of Christ. At times we need to memorize and say repeatedly certain scriptures that give us overcoming power. Our minds need to be filled with thanksgiving for God's promises and provisions. Before the day even begins, we need to acknowledge heartfelt gratefulness to God for His love and provisions and seek His direction for the day.

Finally, we maintain a sound mind by wearing the helmet of salvation. Salvation is the full implementation of covenant with God. Covenant is founded upon repentance, baptism, communion at the Lord's table, tithing and submission to spiritual leadership in God's house. When we are in covenant with God, we have confidence to stand against the wiles of Satan. He loses out in any strategy he tries to throw at us. For one in covenant with God, resisting the devil is not difficult.

> For which I suffer trouble as an evildoer, even to the point of chains; but the word of God is not chained. (2 Timothy 2:9)

I foresee greater attacks than ever before upon the minds of Christians in the days ahead. We cannot possibly be overcomers without having the mind of Christ. His thoughts and direction give us confidence both in offensive and defensive spiritual warfare. We must resist attacks upon our minds, but we must also press into deeper understanding of God's direction through His Word. Spiritual pressing will enable us to withstand social pressures. But remember, spiritual pressing will always create conflicts in our circumstances. Can you drink the cup?

Without the certainty that we are moving according to the mind of Christ, we will never be able to stand against the accusations of Satan. The world believes Satan's lies. But the mind of Christ, a sound mind, a Kingdom mind, will always produce the fruit of righteousness, peace and joy. Such fruit is the manifestation of Kingdom life on earth—the manifestation of the mind of Christ within us, empowered to change the adverse circumstances surrounding us.

A line from an old song we often sing at Chapel Hill Harvester Church gives excellent advice to maintaining a sound mind in a mad, mad world. It says simply, "Build your hopes on things eternal. Hold to God's unchanging hand." Amen and amen!

Chapter Nine
Spiritual Trends

† The maturing bride of Christ will come to know her Bridegroom's personality more and more.

† The concepts of God's nature must be personalized in the Church.

† Covenant teaching will continue to be emphasized in every aspect of ministry in the Church.

† Choices today become a trajectory of life in the eternal state.

† All creation stands at attention to witness the maturity of the *last Eve*, the Church, the bride of Christ.

† Satan tries to tempt the last Eve with the same questions as the first Eve concerning her mission, her strength and her purpose.

† In knowing God, the Church must understand that God is an emotional Being.

† God does not make judgments toward Christians, and especially judgments toward non-Christians, based upon His emotions.

† A Christian views history through the perspective of covenant with the last Eve.

† God's vengeance against unrighteousness is held back at this time by His covenant with man.

† Success defined by a secular view of history stands in sharp contrast to the criteria of success in biblical history.

† In a sudden fall of the world's economy, governments and militaries, the *Day of the Lord* will close the door on those choosing disobedience to God's voice.

† Interaction with God in spirit and truth moves worshipers to a level of communication with God beyond legal obedience to God's written law.

† The last Eve will realize the full meaning of *pleasing God* by fulfilling the Law through the commitment of her heart.

† Relationships among Christians will be resolved as we learn the principles of love by ministering beyond the requirements of the Law.

† In the intimacy of worship, we can share God's compassion, love, anger—His heart.

† God will close the parameters around covenant people's lives (and the lives of their children) as the *Day of the Lord* draws closer.

† Christians who habitually violate their covenant tithing and church attendance—or who do *Christian things* with a sense of obligation—will likely fall away from God in the days ahead.

† Pastors will sense God's emotions over His flock, and must walk a narrow road of accountability for the welfare of the people.

† The last Eve will find the will of God on a matter and pray His will into reality.

† The last Eve must come into an understanding of God's sovereign will through her covenant relationship with the Lord.

† The last Eve must learn what makes God laugh and cry.

† The last Eve will have her eyes opened in extraordinary circumstances.

9

THE RING OF COVENANT

Ministry flows out of relationships. Fitly joined together. One Body. We have examined the Church from various perspectives—its structure in reformation, its mental health in a mad, mad world, its feminine qualities of ministry, its political responsibility and its function in the community. In this world we are identified as *salt* and *light*. But what is our identity to God in the heavenly realm? Who are we to Him? What is the quality of our relationship to Him? The maturing bride will come to know her Bridegroom's personality more and more.

God is good. God is love. How simple that sounds, yet how profound. The most common concepts of God picture Him as a stern judge. We see Him in our minds as a white bearded man with an austere expression on His face sitting upon a throne. He sees and knows everything—particularly the failures, faults and guilt we hide deep within us and had hoped to forget. We can't imagine that He has a sense of humor. Certainly he never tells a joke or feels lonely and needs someone to talk with Him. He's God! How could He feel what we feel?

What is your first reaction at hearing the name, *GOD*? Many Christians have difficulty in accepting a view of a loving heavenly Father Who is also capable of giving orders to wipe out entire cities as He did with Jericho (Joshua 6:21). Yet comprehension of God's personality stretches the finite mind beyond understanding. Imagine a being who has no beginning nor end. Because we live an existence of dimensional relativity, the emotions of an absolute being seem incomprehensible. We struggle over our troubles today while God sees us in the perspective of eternity, all of time merged into a single glance. Our view of eternity is conceptual at best. We comprehend eternity by faith. We accept the reality of eternity beyond our finite understanding.

By faith we believe that once God breathes the breath of life into someone, that person becomes a living soul who will live for eternity. If human beings were able to comprehend an endless existence, everyone would become a Christian. But instead, most people on earth choose to think of life in finite durations—a day, a month, a year, seventy-five years.

Coming into covenant with God inevitably expands our perspective of life's meaning and purpose. Imagine living beyond a million, billion or trillion years. Imagine that the quality of eternity is based upon the choices we have made in this brief span of time comprising our mortal lives. Our choices today become a trajectory into eternity. We live forever with our decisions today, an endless state of reaping the seeds we have sown.

Most people believe that their choices in life are numerous. In reality, life is built on a series of either/or decisions. Yes, we make important choices at plateaus in our lives. We pay attention to decisions at those important moments and remember them. We decide big things like who to marry or what career we will pursue or when to have a baby. But the real essence of who we are and what we are actually is the result of seemingly inconsequential daily decisions. Every day we either move toward covenant with God and the righteousness, peace and joy of His Kingdom, or we move toward rebellion against God by living to please ourselves. No day is unimportant.

Few people realize the magnitude and eternal consequences of their choices. Yet, eternal destiny is determined by the choices of the here and now. In that regard, Satan was correct in telling Eve that the ability to choose between good and evil made her a *little god* over her own destiny (Genesis 3:5). God had created Eve in His image, but her deception and Adam's willful disobedience made redemption through Jesus Christ the only way to know reconciliation with God. Salvation, then, becomes an eternal choice, an act of faith subject to human will and divine law.

The Bible calls Jesus *the last Adam* (1 Corinthians 15:45). Adam was created to be a solution to the chaos resulting from the fall of Lucifer. Man was created as a solution to rebellion. Eve, the mother of creation, was created as a support, a helper to Adam. But her influence in Adam's life became destructive.

The one ray of hope against the penalty of sin over the lives of mankind was God's promise of victory to humanity through the *seed of the woman.* Another Adam (Jesus Christ) would crush the head of the serpent (Genesis 3:15).

Now all creation stands at attention to witness the maturity of the *last Eve,* the Church, the bride of Christ. The last Eve must be the comparable helpmeet to the last Adam. No wonder the Apostle Paul warned the Church to beware of the deception of Eve which is departing from the simplicity that is in Christ (2 Corinthians 11:3). Eve questioned God's instructions in her mind when Satan asked her, "Has God truly spoken?"

Satan tries to tempt the last Eve with the same questions concerning her mission, her strength and her purpose. Satan plants questions concerning the direction of eldership in the body of Christ. Keeping the last Eve in constant derision and confusion delays the culmination of God's plan. Instead of becoming the support to Christ which she is intented to be, the last Eve becomes a selfish lover—controlling, vain and unfulfilling to the Lord of the harvest. She questions His intentions and His directions.

In these important days of destiny, our choices must be deliberate. We will never understand covenant with God until we realize that we have the right to either choose God's will or to pursue an alternate plan. A covenant is an agreement, a contract, a binding marriage relationship. Covenant includes requirements, benefits for those who keep it and even curses for those who violate it. God often spoke to the biblical patriarchs by saying, "If you will . . . then I will . . .", much the way that a man proposes marriage. The heritage of the last Eve—her engagement—began when one man, Abraham, accepted God's offer of covenant. Within three generations (Abraham, Isaac and Jacob), God had called an entire nation into covenant with Him.

Why is covenant with the last Eve important to omnipotent God? Why do we hear so many contemporary Bible teachers emphasizing the necessity of coming into covenant with God? Some say that a Christian's faith will not survive turbulent times of testing without covenant understanding. Is salvation and covenant the same thing? Are all born-again Christians in covenant? What is the meaning of the emphases placed upon covenant families, covenant communities, covenant giving, covenant relationships?

The answers to these questions are hidden in a mystery: the last Adam eagerly anticipates marriage to the last Eve, as a bridegroom rejoices over his bride. One of the most shocking revelations of Scripture is discovering that God is an emotional being. The Kingdom of God is built in trust through covenant. Trust, not love, is the foundation for enduring relationships. For example, the wife of an alcoholic may love her husband, but she certainly can't trust his priorities when his addiction rules his decisions for their family. The Kingdom of God is built in trust.

God distinguishes between those who are in covenant with Him and those who are not in covenant in His dealings with mankind. I will discuss this distinction more in the next chapter. This distinction is dimensional depending upon the obedience of the one in covenant with God. As we press toward the end of the age, human history as we know it, Christians must activate their covenant trust in God. How can the last Eve possibly become a comparable helpmeet to the last Adam unless she knows Him? More than any other analogy of covenant relationship in Scripture, Jesus personifies His role as that of a bridegroom.

I am certain that some people have never thought of God, Who sits upon the throne of all creation, as an emotional being. Many Christians have never considered that God wants to be a husband to them. The Bible proves that He does. Nevertheless, I do not believe that God makes judgments toward Christians, and especially judgments toward non-Christians, based upon His emotions. In fact, the times in Scripture when God acted out of an emotional response of displeasure to events on earth, the Bible says that *He repented* (1 Samuel 15:35 OKJ). Because God is emotional, God makes a covenant—an agreement of trust—with the last Eve based on mutual respect for the terms of their agreement.

Allow me to illustrate the difference between an emotional response and a response of covenant by using a personal example. Sometimes as a senior pastor I am confronted with problems concerning members of my staff. Perhaps a staff member's work productivity has hit a slump, and his negligence is affecting other workers. I will try to avoid making any decisions about that staff member based upon my emotional response to this person. If I have particularly strong emotions—positively or negatively—toward that staff member, I will likely back away from making any decision whatsoever. Instead, I will call my Presbytery to come to a joint decision in the best interest of that staff member and other workers affected by that person.

Justice demands objectivity. An emotional response is highly subjective. Because a just God has a strong emotional response to the last Eve, He has established a criterion of objectivity for Himself in His dealings with all mankind—believers and unbelievers alike. Rain falls on the just and the unjust (Matthew 5:45). God placed a rainbow in the heavens as a sign of His covenant promise that He would not destroy the earth again by water (Genesis 9:11-17).

Covenant with God is a fixed law on which mankind can depend. God's Word is unchangeable truth. God's covenant with man represents a standard of His fixed law. Nevertheless, God, the perfection of justice and righteousness, unchangeable in His covenant promises, is an emotional being. One of the most crucial tests of maturity for the last Eve is discerning the dimensions of God's personality—His law, His covenant, His emotions. The first Eve was created to be joined to Adam. Together they reflect the image of God to all creation. The last Eve is to be joined to the last Adam as a joint heir of all things.

THE GOD OF HISTORY

What are the distinctions of God's personality? God grew angry with Israel when she turned to idolatry in the wilderness. An angry God declared His intention of destroying the obstinate Hebrews and starting again with a new group. Moses interceded for the people. The prophet reminded God of His covenant with Abraham. Moses reasoned with God concerning the heathens' perspective if Israel perished (Exodus 32:12-14). Moses even insisted that God blot him out, too, if He took vengeance on Israel. The Bible says, "So the Lord relented [repented] from the harm which He said He would do to His people" (Exodus 32:14).

Of course love is an emotion, and the Bible

defines God as *Love* (1 John 4:8). Love without emotion is impossible. Yet if God always dealt with mankind in accordance with His loving nature, He would override justice and His fixed laws of retribution. I am certain that in His love for mankind, God would never allow AIDS to destroy innocent people's lives. According to His loving nature, God would never allow powerful nuclear weapons to destroy life on the planet He created in such beauty.

But, instead of controlling us according to His emotions, God allows us the freedom to choose His will for ourselves. An individual's calling in history is determined by God's sovereign purposes for His bride. Everyone wants to know three basic things about himself: Where did I come from? What is my purpose in life? Where am I going? This search for personal identity is resolved by the way we identify our role in history—more specifically, God's plan for the last Eve.

God's covenant laws are fixed principles. People who sow kindness, reap kindness (Galatians 6:7-9). The way of the unfaithful [transgressor] is hard (Proverbs 13:15). God has established His laws. He holds to His unchangeable Word regardless of His emotional response. For the covenant Christian, history represents a trajectory of spiritual promises passed down through generations, ending in the total reconciliation of all things—the marriage of the last Adam and the last Eve (Ephesians 1:10).

And what is the historical perspective of unbelievers? A person who disregards covenant with God as the criterion for identity views his place in history in terms of self-serving goals. Science, economics, politics, philosophy, all these can become godlike to one who makes decisions in life based upon a secular

view of history. I contend that all people have a religion, even if it is atheism, agnosticism, humanism or
patriotism. Humanistic values appear to be very noble, but they are actually transitory and self-serving.
Ultimately, all is *vanity* for the humanist except
whatever achievements he can leave for the next
generation to enjoy. At best a humanistic view of
death is rather bleak.

No one exemplifies more self-confidence than a
person who is able to state specifically his purpose in
life. Goals are related to one's purpose in life, but
goals and purpose are not the same. A person's purpose determines his goals. Purpose and identity are
synonymous. Only in covenant do we comprehend
God's purposes. Covenant with God, then, is the key
to discovering one's identity. Once a Christian begins
to identify himself as a part of *the last Eve,* only then
can he begin to know God's heart, God as an emotional being—beyond law, beyond grace.

Peter describes God as *longsuffering,* which is an
emotion (2 Peter 3:9). But God will not wait forever.
When God's purposes are finally fulfilled, God will
act. The *fullness of time* (Galatians 4:4) indicates
that God knows the designated fulfillment of His
witness which calls for an emotional response from
Him. The Bible refers to the *time of harvest,* then the
end of the age. A particular season of history is identified because of its relevance to God's plan for the
last Eve. Covenant promises assure us that God will
never again act against unrighteousness as He did in
Noah's day:

> Then the Lord saw that the wickedness of man was
> great in the earth, and that every intent of the thoughts
> of his heart was only evil continually. And the Lord was
> sorry that He had made man on the earth, and He was

grieved in His heart. So the Lord said, "I will destroy man whom I have created from the face of the earth, both man and beast, creeping thing and birds of the air, for I am sorry that I have made them." But Noah found grace in the eyes of the Lord. (Genesis 6:5-8)

Imagine the emotional response of God's grieving because He had made man. We can be thankful that God does not deal with humanity on the basis of His emotions, rather than on the basis of His covenant. Imagine God's emotions as He watches drug traffic, child pornography, people starving to death while other people live near them in luxury.

Like Moses' intercession before God on behalf of the Hebrews in the wilderness, Abraham also interceded on behalf of his nephew, Lot, and his family who lived in the depraved city of Sodom and Gomorrah. As strange as this account seems to us as we read it, Abraham actually bargained with God to spare the city (Genesis 18:23-32). Undoubtedly, God's emotions are just as vehement against the wickedness of cities today. What holds back God's vengeance?

PROTECTION UNDER COVENANT

Covenant is based upon predetermined stipulations governing relationships and response. For example, in human relationships a parent follows certain predetermined laws of discipline in correcting his children. Otherwise, an angry parent could physically or emotionally harm a child who has misbehaved. That parent's predetermined law of protecting the child's health and welfare override what could be the parent's emotional reaction of justifiable anger.

Scripture indicates that God is moved with emotion at hearing the cries of departed saints under the altar, "How long, O Lord . . . until You judge . . .?" (Revelation 6:10). God feels the heartache of people in confusion, crying to Him for answers. God feels angry toward every form of satanic oppression—in world markets, in government, in religion, in family relationships. God must remind Himself of the *Day of the Lord* when He will vent His wrath against all forces of darkness (Joel 3:2). But for now God backs away. He relies on intercessors' prayers, agreement of heaven and earth, to act in behalf of the saints. His vengeance against unrighteousness is constrained presently by His own Word to His covenant people.

Meanwhile, skeptics of this world say continually, ". . . All things continue as they were . . ." (2 Peter 3:3,4). Secular historians disregard prophetic insights and the influence of the Church. Success defined by a secular view of history stands in sharp contrast to the criteria of success in biblical history. The patriarchs of faith listed in Hebrews (Chapter 11) would hardly be candidates for a secular *Hall of Fame* which focuses on wealth, achievement, power and might.

Since the days of Noah, mankind has never seen the consequences of God's wrath. We have only seen devastation as a result of sin, mankind sowing to the flesh. Disobedience to God's will has caused wars, famine, pollution, disease and pestilence. But God has held back His hand from judgment of sin. Sin serves as its own judge in that it inevitably causes devastation. The wages of sin is death (Romans 6:23). God's judgment for the sins of the world is yet to come.

The Bible speaks of a specific time when Babylon will fall (Revelation 18:21). The *Day of the Lord* will cause islands to be removed and the earth to reel like a drunkard (Isaiah 24:20). Imagine the sudden fall of the world's economy, governments and militaries. Just as God closed the door of the ark with only Noah and his family safe within, the *Day of the Lord* will close the door on those choosing disobedience to God's voice. The Bible says that God *hates* disobedience.

> These six things the Lord hates, yes, seven are an abomination to Him: A proud look, a lying tongue, hands that shed innocent blood, a heart that devises wicked plans, feet that are swift in running to evil, a false witness who speaks lies, and one who sows discord among brethren. (Proverbs 6:16-19)

Why does God hate these things? Vanity is the fruit of a proud heart. Giving too much attention to the flesh instead of the spiritual man directs one away from pleasing God. Vanity opens a person to deception. Vanity is one of the major temptations for the last Eve. We live in a star-studded society. That stardom spirit brings mixture into the house of the Lord.

God in His longsuffering nature withholds judgment. God hates liars, who usually are entangled by their own sin. Shedding innocent blood can as easily refer to making false accusations against someone as it does to committing acts of physical violence.

Devising wicked plans results from an evil imagination. The entertainment industry plants many seeds of wickedness in the minds of multitudes of people today. Feet that run to evil represent those who enjoy gossip, bad reports, gambling casinos, pornography, etc. Some people are drawn to evil and feel comfortable in darkness.

Finally, God hates one who causes strife among brethren. Because this problem has become such a widespread hindrance in the lives of many Christians today, I have written a book on the subject of Christian unity, *That the World May Know* (Kingdom Publishers, 1987). I believe that God is sounding a trumpet of unity in the body of Christ today.

People often ask, "Why doesn't a righteous God do something about those who make Him angry?" The answer is *covenant!* God's purpose, design and unbending promises enable us to depend upon His grace. We live in the day of God's grace extended toward us—until the *Day of the Lord,* until the fullness of time. However, grace does not automatically mean that Christians share the concerns of God's heart merely because we keep His law and receive His provisions. Only those who share God's emotional nature enter into His presence and realize the desires of His heart. Many sit among the bride without wearing the appropriate wedding garments.

Worship is communion with God. Worship touches God's emotions. We acknowledge His covenant and His Law as we enter into His presence in the outer courts of thanksgiving and praise. As we move into the inner court and into God's inner chambers, we share heart-to-heart communion with God. The Law does not change in the inner courts. God has determined the laws of His sovereign will and has established them, even for Himself. But interaction with God in spirit and truth moves worshipers to a level of communication beyond legal obedience to God's laws. God's laws are written upon our hearts—we want to please Him. Laws written upon our hearts prevent us from even having a desire to sin. The Holy Spirit works conviction within us.

PLEASING GOD

Until we share the emotional dimension of God's nature, we'll never realize the full meaning of *pleasing God*. Beyond the Law is reverence, thanksgiving and adoration of God, a heartfelt desire to please Him which becomes the motivation for all decisions of life. Some people pray with the realization that they bring pleasure to God. Though God's Law does not change for true worshipers, their sensitivity to His laws and His nature intensifies their desire to be obedient. Intimacy with God brings confidence and strength to carry out God's will in any test.

The covenant of marriage ensures certain rights in the lives of a husband and his wife. Civil law will uphold the marriage contract as binding. Nevertheless, a marriage held together on the basis of legal rights alone is an unfulfilling relationship. Emotions of passion, loyalty and tenderness are not required by law in the marriage contract. The heart and the spirit determine pleasure in marriage. When physical attraction is not coupled with mature emotional commitment, even the physical relationship is not satisfying for very long. Intimacy involves emotional interaction in both human relationships as well as in our relationship with God.

God said of Jesus, "This is My beloved Son, in whom I am well pleased" (Matthew 3:17). This statement was not spoken as a Father commending His Son on keeping the Law. God's pleasure in His Son was the result of Jesus' sensitivity to His Father's voice. Jesus is the perfect example of spiritual obedience as a response to God's love—the emotional nature of God.

Likewise, to please God, the last Eve must minister beyond the requirements of the Law. Why did

Jesus say that harlots and publicans enter the Kingdom before upright Pharisees? Their hearts were tenderized by Jesus' forgiveness. They responded to His compassion and grace. They were released from bondages when He touched them. They received His healing love, and then they became a channel of that love to others in need.

People who tithe do not please God. The Bible simply calls those who fail to keep this requirement *thieves* (Malachi 3:8). People who want to please God in financial matters sow seed in good ground, ministries that demonstrate the Kingdom of God. Offerings beyond the tithe please God because such willingness to give to God's cause demonstrates faith in God's law of "give, and you shall receive." A *cheerful* giver moves into the realm of emotions, beyond legal requirements. They please God with their response from their hearts.

The Law says, "Do not kill." People who refrain from committing murder when they are angry do not please God. God is pleased whenever someone with justifiable anger releases the hatred in his heart for God to change those destructive feelings. Then he moves by faith into the realm of communion with God's emotions—forgiving as God forgives. He directs his trust toward God rather than *taking up the sword* against an offender. Such trust pleases God. Pleasing God means going an extra mile if someone requires that we walk one mile with him while carrying his belongings. Pleasing God means turning the other cheek when someone slaps or abuses us for no reason.

Covenant with God takes us beyond the requirements of the Law. The last Eve enters the emotional realm of interaction with the Holy Spirit. Praying early in the morning, studying God's Word daily—

these are not required by God, but the benefits are manifold. A loving wife's thoughtful response to her husband may not be required, but such affection results in his seeking ways to please her also.

Some people seek for ways to please God. The Bible says that without faith, it is impossible to please Him (Hebrews 11:6). Some Christians keep covenant with God—tithing, attending church, baptism, celebrating the Lord's Supper, honoring spiritual headship—but still fail to walk so that they please God beyond the requirements of the Law.

Imagine how many relationships would be resolved if people understood that pleasing God means entering an emotional realm of interaction beyond the requirements of the Law. This spiritual principle also applies in natural relationships. We do have the ability to feel as God feels to some degree, at least to differentiate between acts that meet requirements and acts resulting from the emotion of love. A mother who merely feeds, protects and shelters her children will not meet their needs without also sharing loving, emotional interaction with them.

> Beloved, if our heart does not condemn us, we have confidence toward God. And whatever we ask we receive from Him, because we keep His commandments and do those things that are pleasing in His sight. (1 John 3:21,22)

How do we know what pleases God? First, we must know God's character. The Old Testament is especially valuable in giving insights into the character of God. Those who love justice and mercy please God. Jesus said, "Woe to you, scribes and Pharisees, hypocrites! For you pay tithe of mint and anise and cummin, and have neglected the weightier matters of the law: justice and mercy and faith. These you ought to have done, without leaving the others undone" (Matthew 23:23).

When someone commits an offense against us, we are not required to show mercy. No wonder God finds such pleasure in one who judges with a heart of mercy. God is pleased with someone who stays in a marriage and trusts God when they are justified in getting a divorce. Paul emphasized that a mature Christian stays in a troubled marriage in order to redeem the weaker partner. Too difficult?

No one is more compassionate toward divorced people than I am. I have pastors on my Presbytery and staff members who are divorced. Nevertheless, the divorce rate of our nation is an abomination. Few adults in our society understand giving beyond the requirements of the law. We can expect the divorce rate, the single parent families and the children born to unwed mothers to continue to rise in the secular world. But what about the accelerating divorce rate among Christian couples? We must learn the secret of pleasing God beyond the requirements of the law.

How many children's lives would be revolutionized if parents would extend mercy beyond the letter of the law to understand their children's basic needs. Compassion is learned best through experience. Few people learn the meaning of *compassion* by reading the definition in a dictionary. Those who give mercy receive mercy. Imagine the atmosphere of a home where the family extended mercy and justice beyond that which was required by the rules of that household. What kind of children would come from a home like that? They would minister to others spontaneously, without any hesitation. Ministry and edification would flow naturally from them.

EMOTIONAL INTERACTION

Obviously, a mature bride will interact with her husband in the realm of his emotions. Likewise, the last Eve, the bride of Christ, must interact with God in an emotional realm. While we keep the covenant and the Law (Thou shall not kill; Thou shall not steal; Thou shall not lie . . .) we begin to realize that true blessings from God come from pleasing Him beyond merely strict adherence to His Laws. Blessings come in abundance when we become God's pleasure. The Apostle John heard the heavenly hosts singing that we were created for the *pleasure* of God (Revelation 4:11).

Anger is an emotion which God expressed in the Old Testament. "And the Lord was very angry with Aaron and would have destroyed him . . ." (Deuteronomy 9:20). Notice the words, ". . . would have destroyed . . ." That phraseology indicates God's emotional response.

In His anger God wanted the golden calf ground up, thrown in the brook and the children of Israel to be forced to drink the water. Moses depicted God's anger by taking the tablets of the Law and dashing them to the ground. Then out of covenant God spoke to Moses and repented of His emotional reaction to the sin of idolatry.

The modern Church focuses on God's love and compassion. I'm sure many Christians are uncomfortable admitting that God's anger could be kindled against them. But unless we know the Lord as an emotional being, we can never become the mature bride who will rule and reign with Christ. We lack the understanding to share God's heart in intercession. We fail to take authority in the name of the Lord when we share God's righteous indignation against wrongdoing. Instead, we remain immature in faith and in our relationship with the Lord.

In His anger God warned Solomon twice against honoring other gods and causing mixture in his household through intermarriage. God finally told Solomon that because he had not kept God's covenant and statutes, He would tear the kingdom of Israel from his house and give it to his servant (1 Kings 11:9-13). Notice that God continues to honor His covenant with David by not destroying the tribe completely. Covenant with David was binding to God, superceding His emotional response to Solomon's spiritual transgressions within his household.

Once we understand how covenant protects mankind from the emotions of God, we are able to relate to Him in the realm of His emotions and keep His Law. The Law is given as an objective, immovable guide for human behavior in God's Kingdom. God's Law is our standard for living. But God's pleasure becomes those Christians who love His Law in both spirit and truth. In that realm we share intimacy with God in worship. We share His compassion, love, anger—His heart.

Imagine how God searches the earth for a people who desire to please Him! Pleasing God is the meaning of *blessing* Him. People who *bless the Lord* do not focus on spiritual *requirements* and *paying dues* to God or to the Church. They seek ways to honor the Lord, drawing closer to Him, serving Him with all their hearts.

The Bible also says that God is a jealous God. ". . . You shall not bow down to them [idols] nor serve them. For I, the Lord your God, am a jealous God, visiting the iniquity of the fathers on the children to the third and fourth generations of those who hate

Me . . ." (Exodus 20:5). God not only admits to feeling jealousy, He sternly warns people of the consequences of His jealousy over them. God demands that He alone be worshiped as God. Many people do not want to admit that God makes this disclosure of His personality.

I believe that the devastation in many people's lives is the result of God's jealousy over them. He will not allow subsequent generations of covenant people to transgress His laws. The children of godly parents often receive what appears to be harsh circumstances as the result of their sins—seemingly more severe than the children of unbelievers. Why? God is jealous over them. They are living under the binding laws of covenant made with their parents in their behalf. God will allow devastation in their lives to draw them back to Him. He is a jealous God!

As I stated previously, most people believe that they have unlimited choices in life, including the ability to disregard God's calling and purposes in creating them. The Bible teaches that God closes the parameters around people's lives as the fullness of time draws near. Yes, God is longsuffering. Yes, God always honors His Law. But judgment begins at the house of God (1 Peter 4:17). God's judgments against disobedience are first visited upon people who understand salvation, Kingdom standards, Jesus' commission to His Church. We see that judgment meted out increasingly in our day.

We live in the dawning of the *Day of the Lord.* We think we've seen some shocking events in modern history. We haven't seen anything yet! Christians will not survive the days ahead without fully implementing their covenants with God and embracing His purposes for their lives with a desire to please

Him. Christians who habitually violate their covenant tithing and church attendance—or who do
Christian things with a sense of obligation—will
likely fall away from God in the days ahead. They
will wake up suddenly and wonder where they
missed out!

A pastor called by God feels the emotions of God
over his people in this hour. Sometimes that emotion
is anger at seeing stubborn disobedience and unbelief. Pastors are certainly angry at Satan's deception
of people who turn away from truth. People often are
tricked into believing that they will *get by*. I also
sense a growing awareness within many pastors who
recognize their own accountability for their people as
the *Day of the Lord* draws near. Ministers must walk
a narrow road in seeking the Lord's direction on
behalf of the flock.

Who will be able to stand in the great and terrible *Day of the Lord?* Babylon will fall. Who will
stand? The last Eve—Christians who understand
covenant with God and live as His pleasure—will
stand. We must release our souls and minds to be
conformed to God's will. Jealousy, for example, is
proper both in marriage and in parent-child relationships when the emotional involvement results in protection and provision. In this sense, jealousy—which
is often destructive—is a positive and proper emotion.
Improper jealousy kills, steals and destroys others,
while proper jealousy protects and brings life to others by releasing them to God's purposes.

JESUS' EMOTIONS

What was Jesus' emotion as He drove out the
moneychangers from the temple (Matthew 21:12)? It
was anger, of course. One way we can discern the

righteousness of our emotions is to compare our feelings to those Jesus seemed to have in various situations. Today God's anger is kindled against those who use people in the house of God to increase profits in their businesses. Some sell trinkets that supposedly help one to come into prosperity or health. Some people join churches because they see the members as perspective clients for their businesses. That motivation angers God, the same way that the moneychangers who saw people hungering for the Lord as an opportunity to make money, angered Jesus to the point of lashing out at them with a whip.

In Jesus' day poor people bought sacrifices from these merchandisers who would increase the price since the poor were forced to buy from them. The moneychangers took advantage of people by using their spiritual hunger to make money. What was God's emotion toward this practice? Jesus braided the whip, turned over tables and called the moneychangers *thieves!* Out of emotions of intense anger, Jesus demonstrated God's response to such merchandising opportunists.

Jesus saw a multitude of people, and He was moved with compassion because they were scattered like sheep without a shepherd (Matthew 9:36-38). He felt their restlessness and confusion. He wanted to help them find answers to the hopelessness they felt. They were lost and afraid. Jesus instructed His disciples to pray for laborers to minister to the multitude of people who were seeking for guidance.

A man came to Jesus for Him to heal a son who fell on the ground with epileptic seizures (Mark 9:14-25). Jesus looked straight into the father's eyes and said, "If you can believe, all things are possible . . ." The father responded, "Lord, I believe, [but the circumstances are so grave and have been like this for so long] help my unbelief!" Jesus acted with great compassion at the honesty of this man's answer. The man's emotions were genuine—not religious pretention nor demands. His heart was humble; therefore, Jesus could respond to his cry for help.

A Canaanite woman asked Jesus to heal her daughter. He replied sharply, "I was not sent except to the lost sheep of the house of Israel" (Matthew 15:24). But the woman was persistent. Her faith enabled her to see the big picture of Who Jesus was. Her reply to Jesus implied, "But Master, beyond the Law of Your mission to Israel is God's love for the world which includes everyone—even dogs feeding on the crumbs that fall from the table." Jesus responded to her faith and healed her daughter. His emotions reached beyond the Law of His primary mission to redeem the house of Israel to one understanding His mission to the world.

If only Christians could respond to one another beyond the requirements of the Law. If we could only end our thinking toward one another in terms of what someone owes us or what obligations we are expected to meet to prove we are followers of Christ. People easily open their hearts to acts of love extended to them beyond those which they expect Christians to do. True ministers of the Lord understand that principle and they flow in mercy and grace toward others. Peter exemplified that spirit when he told Jesus, "Lord, not my feet only, but also my hands and my head!" (John 13:9). Peter was saying, "I want all of You that I can receive—beyond the basic requirements for cleansing!"

THE LAST EVE'S ENGAGEMENT

So what is the ring of covenant? How prepared is the last Eve for her wedding? Jesus wants to be a bridegroom, a husband to His Church. He wants us to willingly give ourselves to Him in marriage—body (Romans 12:1), soul (John 15:14) and spirit (John 16:13). Such a commitment brings the Church into intimacy with God through continuous interaction with Him. As the *Day of the Lord* draws closer and the bride of Christ is manifested as a witness to all nations, these are the ways in which the last Eve will move in ministry as the betrothed, one wearing the ring of covenant:

The last Eve will find God's direction on a matter and pray His will into reality. Jesus' instruction for us to pray, ". . . Your Kingdom come, Your will be done on earth as it is in heaven" is not a simple prayer to implement. Intercession calls for emotional interaction with God. Yes, the Holy Bible, read by anyone who is literate, states God's will. But what is the meaning of *fervent prayer* in intercession if agreement with God is simply a matter of stating aloud the things God has spoken in His Word by giving intellectual assent?

Binding and loosing in intercession calls for a combination of faith, love and confidence that we are speaking into the atmosphere the specific will of God. We become trumpets of Kingdom proclamation in intercession. The creative word from God's heart is spoken with our mouths in His name. Then circumstances opposing God's will begin to change according to God's plan.

The last Eve must come into an understanding of God's sovereign will through her covenant relationship with the Lord. Each person was created for a specific purpose in the Kingdom of God. Fulfillment comes in giving our lives individually to those purposes for which we were created. To be in God's plan for our lives prepares us for rulership in the Kingdom of God. We are royalty in training. We are destined for the throne. That throne is servanthood—he who serves, leads. But a good servant must respond to his master's voice. We have assignments from God for which we are accountable.

Serving in God's plan, living in God's will, assures us of all the covenant promises for ourselves and for our children. God's loving protection and provision are given to us according to His unchangeable law (Psalm 91). Covenant is tested by pressure to conform to this world. We have warfare, but God also provides the weapons to fight the good fight, to be overcomers, to be more than conquerors through Jesus Christ.

The last Eve must learn what makes God laugh. The Psalmist wrote that God laughs at men who plot against Him (Psalm 2:4). How comforting! God must be amazed that evil men think they can stand against Him. Remember, He sees the whole picture from beginning to end—all of history at a single glance. Only God can say to those in covenant, ". . . I will give You the nations for Your inheritance, and the ends of the earth for Your possession" (Psalm 2:8).

> The wicked plots against the just, and gnashes at him with his teeth. The Lord laughs at him, for He sees that his day is coming. (Psalm 37:12,13)

Reward and punishment are found in God's law and covenant with man. God laughs at those who violate His will and think they will escape retribution. Babylon will fall, and those who have put their trust in world systems will fall with it.

> God shall likewise destroy you forever; He shall take you away, and pluck you out of your dwelling place, and uproot you from the land of the living. Selah. The righteous also shall see and fear, and *shall laugh* at him, saying, "Here is the man who did not make God his strength, but trusted in the abundance of his riches, and strengthened himself in his wickedness." (Psalm 52:5-7)

It is not coincidental that so many scriptures dealing with God's laughter are found in the Psalms. David was a fugitive on the run from King Saul and his men who were determined to kill him. Men motivated by flesh always seek to kill God's anointed ones. Perhaps it seems strange to us who feel the unpleasant repercussions of such evil devices waged against us, but hearing men's evil plots makes God laugh:

> Indeed, they belch out with their mouth; Swords are in their lips; For they say, "Who hears?" But You, O Lord, shall *laugh* at them . . . (Psalm 59:7,8)

Is it possible for the bride of Christ to laugh also at the devil's attempts to stop the move of God across the earth? What confidence in knowing, ". . . The earth will be filled with the knowledge of the glory of the Lord, as the waters cover the sea" (Habakkuk 2:14). The joy of the Lord is our strength. Satan is a defeated foe.

The last Eve must learn what makes God cry. Jesus was a high priest who was touched with the feelings of our infirmities (Hebrews 4:15). Whereas I picture Jesus laughing with children, His disciples and the people as He taught them, we have a less vivid account in Scripture of Jesus' laughter than we do of His tears.

Jesus cried at the tomb of his friend, Lazarus, as he realized personally the sting of man's sin against God resulting in human death (John 11:35). He wept over Jerusalem, perhaps the most painful words which He uttered, because Israel refused her time of visitation (Luke 19:41-44). Jesus' emotion of sorrow in the Garden of Gethsemane where He said that His "soul was exceedingly sorrowful, even to death," indicates the deep sorrow of His manhood as He faced betrayal and death on the cross (Mark 14:33,34).

What are the reasons that the bride of Christ cries as she shares the Bridegroom's tears? Division among Christians. Death where God wants to bring life. People refusing a visitation of God. People closed to truth. These are the reasons that God cries today. He is long-suffering and great in His mercy toward us, but a day of reckoning will come. He will dry the tears from our eyes, and we will know everlasting joy.

The last Eve must learn to seek truth with all her heart. Knowing truth does not come easily. Jesus said to seek, knock, ask, search, buy, hear, do—all active verbs related to knowing truth from God. Knowing truth takes total dedication because we can easily become distracted, delayed, or even deceived. Many Christians play theological games, proving their points and thinking that by intellect, research and clever combinations of Scripture, they can win in theological debate. Perhaps they win an argument, but do they know truth? Jesus said, "I am truth."

Truth is found in God's Holy Word. The Holy Spirit guides us into all truth (John 16:13). Our worship must be pure before God, in Spirit and in truth

(John 4:23). To know truth is to know God, but as you learn of Him, get ready for some surprises. He's not a stern judge without loving compassion. He says for us to come to Him for rest—His yoke (covenant, marriage) is easy, and His burden (concerns, assignments) is light (victory over all obstacles). He knows our frame. He warns us of the problems, and then assures us of the solutions. He says to us:

> . . . These things I have spoken to you, that in Me you may have peace. In the world you will have tribulation; but be of good cheer, I have overcome the world. (John 16:33)

Get ready to have your eyes opened in extraordinary circumstances. The last Eve will be feeding the hungry or visiting those in prison, and she'll suddenly realize, *Why, this is Jesus!* She'll sense unexplainable emotions and realize suddenly, *This is the way God sees this person, this circumstance, this problem.* A world is dying without hope unless people hear the gospel of the Kingdom. Those who are God's pleasure, those who share the intimacy of His emotions in covenant relationship with Him, will minister righteousness, peace and joy in His name. The last Eve is a comparable helpmeet to the last Adam, and people in darkness to whom we extend our hands of love will look into the face of the bride and say with recognition, "Yes, now I see Jesus!"

Chapter Ten
Spiritual Trends

† God will allow some of the most committed Christians in the Church to face major warfare in the days ahead to answer the challenge of the devil.

† Overcoming the tactics of spiritual warfare will bring the bride of Christ to maturity.

† The Church will learn the difference between warfare for righteousness' sake and the consequences of disobedience to God's will.

† The Church will learn to fight with spiritual weapons at a greater dimension.

† We are entering the time of separation of wheat and tares within the Church. Pressures of life will separate them.

† Purity of witness will come to the Church as God judges mixture in individuals and in the Christian community.

† Mixture in the Church will surface in our attitudes toward the secular media, the mind of reason versus the mind of the Spirit, finances, theological debate on the printed page, the *passing of the baton* in ministry, the *old guard* versus the *new guard* in leadership and church structure—especially in regard to the ministry of apostles and prophets.

† The Church will learn to trust God beyond its understanding of circumstances as we endure great persecution.

† Signs, wonders and miracles will increase in the ministry of the Church as interaction with ministering spirits accelerates in visible demonstration.

† The martyr spirit will cause the Church to overcome by the blood of the Lamb, the Word of our testimony and loving not our lives unto death.

† God is ready to deal harshly with those in His house who have "trampled the blood of Christ" underfoot. God is saying, "Don't even pray for them any longer."

† Destructive insiders in the Church will inflict the greatest persecution against God's true bride. Their deception will sound *spiritual* enough to convince many to turn away from God's will.

† Destructive insiders will be characterized by self-righteous arrogance and a lack of repentance.

† God will judge destructive insiders at the same time that the true bride is purged of mixture.

† The Church will learn that the secret of endurance in persecution is staying in covenant with God.

† The Church will not bend under pressure as weapons formed against her are turned on her accusers.

10

THE HEDGE

Jesus compared world conditions in the last days to life in the days of Noah. I believe that He was referring to people who are spiritually deaf and blind, a condition so evident in modern society. Cares of this world close people's hearts to hearing God's warnings.

I can relate many instances in the Word of the Lord in which men asked God, "Will the people hear?" I believe that messengers often experience painful rejection when people resist the words God gives them to speak. I have asked the Lord to make me spiritually strong so that any resistance to a message from Him will only challenge my spirit to proclaim

His Word with greater boldness.

Sometimes messengers go to people who will not receive the message. One principle is certain. Judgment is determined according to whether one opens or closes his will to God's Word. Jesus' words forced all who heard him to make eternal choices. God sends His witnesses, then judgment falls. Often God prepares the messenger for the resistance he will encounter. God said to Ezekiel,

> But the house of Israel will not listen to you, because they will not listen to Me; for all the house of Israel are impudent and hard-hearted. Behold, I have made your face strong against their faces, and your forehead against their foreheads. Like adamant stone, harder than flint, I have made your forehead; do not be afraid of them, nor be dismayed at their looks, though they are a rebellious house. (Ezekiel 3:7-9)

Often I ask my congregation to touch their ears to anoint their hearing before we open God's Word together. That little exercise—touching their ears—is an act of faith. An anointed word from the Lord which falls on deaf ears is lost.

God is giving direction to His Church today which demands great spiritual maturity. The most profound directions from the Lord will seem foolish to your natural understanding. Christians will be unable to demonstrate the witness God desires for His Church unless we allow the Holy Spirit to purge our motivations, relationships and goals. Purging is painful and costly from the perspective of human nature. Though all who have received Jesus Christ as Savior are members of His body and heirs of salvation, Christian commitment varies among believers.

If you are a Christian who seeks first the Kingdom of God with all your heart and comprehends the life and death ramifications of entering into covenant with God, you will live on the cutting edge of Christian witness. You will know great peril, heartache and misunderstanding from the people closest to you. But mixture remaining in any area of your life will hinder implementing the purposes of God both for you and for the corporate Church in this critical hour.

Satan is having a final fling in the lives of many Christians today. *Fling* is defined as *a time of unrestrained pleasure or dissipation.* While I agree with many Bible teachers who say that Satan will grow stronger in power before the coming of Christ, I don't intend to focus on Satan's influence in terms of biblical eschatology. I have very strong opinions about the interpretation of passages referring to the end of the age. Allow me simply to call the period of Satan's final fling *the harvest time.* Few Christians would dispute that we are now in the time of harvest. The focus of this message is on the unprecedented struggle facing Christians who are dedicated laborers in the harvest of the Lord.

GOD REMOVES THE HEDGE

The book of Job depicts a prototype of the Church and gives profound insights into the witness of the Church in the world today. The parallels between Job's circumstances and those of covenant Christians go step by step throughout this story. Accusations of Satan against Job and the warfare in Job's circumstances so symbolize the struggles in the Church, both in individual lives and in the corporate body of Christ. Without this insight into the dimensions of warfare, the problems and struggles of saints

269

seeking the Kingdom of God with all their hearts call God's goodness and love into question.

God said to Satan, "Have you considered My servant Job?" God could say as well, "Satan, have you considered My Church? While the systems of the world are following mammon and educational institutions are advocating humanism, My Church relies upon her covenant with Me. She is seeking Me with all her heart. There is nothing like My Church!"

> So Satan answered the Lord and said, "Does Job fear God for nothing? Have You not made a hedge around him, around his household, and around all that he has on every side? You have blessed the work of his hands, and his possessions have increased in the land . . ." (Job 1:9,10)

Covenant people live with a spiritual hedge surrounding their lives and possessions (Psalm 91). That hedge of protection can only be removed by divine will and purpose of God, or by your willingly stepping out from behind God's protection through acts of disobedience. Disobedience to God's will always cuts off God's ability to bless you. Though disobedience may seem pleasurable for a season, the final result is always destruction. Disobedient people take themselves outside of God's covering by making their own choices.

> But now, stretch out Your hand and touch all that he has, and he will surely curse You to Your face! (Job 1:11)

God always has the ability to limit Satan's operation in your life. God's hedge around you is real, and His removing the hedge to strengthen you by allowing trials is just as real. The temptation to blame

God—always a blaring voice of temptation in your mind in times of adversity—actually was spoken to Job through his wife. Sometimes the most unlikely people, those whom you dearly love, become the vessels through whom you will receive temptations and torment. When the hedge is lowered by God, Satan strikes with the most powerful weapons he can find. Whereas the character of God is love, the character of Satan is destruction—to kill, steal and destroy.

God is lowering the hedge from around the most anointed ministries in the world today because Satan has challenged God concerning their covenant with Him. Too many times our Christian commitment is based upon benefits, prosperity and blessings from God. Satan has said to God, "If you will let me infiltrate their camp and turn me loose to a greater dimension, I will cause them to back away from You."

Many Christians do not want to hear the warning that their commitment will be tested. They reject that message and the messenger. Nevertheless, warfare is a necessary ingredient in producing the kind of witness which God requires His Church to become. Our witness is not only to the world, but more importantly, we witness to powers and principalities of the air (Ephesians 6:12).

A person who is disobedient to God is not in warfare; he is in disobedience. You must discern the difference between disobedience to God's will and true spiritual warfare. Outside of God's will, a Christian inevitably experiences great devastation. The way of a transgressor is always hard. But even within God's perfect will for your life, people called and chosen by the Lord will know tremendous spiritual warfare as we approach the coming of the Lord.

271

Why? Warfare produces maturity. Disobedience produces devastation which hopefully will lead one to repentance. Your actions in life and death situations depend upon your knowing the difference between the consequences of disobedience and the promises of conquest in spiritual warfare. Too often Christians believe they are in warfare when they are really disobedient to God's direction.

The prodigal son was not experiencing warfare when he decided to return to his father's house; he was in disobedience to his covenant relationship with his father. He left his covenant to live his own way and eventually found himself in the pigpen of life. Then he realized that he had been a fool.

The prodigal son reactivated his covenant with his father by saying, "I am no longer worthy to be called your son." In the son's humility, the father responded by calling for the best robe, sandals and a ring for his son to wear. The father ordered a celebration saying, "My son was dead and now he is alive again. He was lost, but now he is found."

While the son was in the pigpen, he was in transgression against his father and lived in total disobedience. At first he enjoyed riotous living, but then he suffered because of his sin. But as soon as the son returned to covenant with his father and received the ring of authority, he entered true warfare. The older brother would not go to the celebration because he was angry. He criticized his brother and complained to his father.

Why is God lowering the hedge which protects covenant Christians? Understand that the hedge is lowered only for those in covenant with God—those who have the testimony of Job. In total obedience to God, you will always stand under great attack. God says to you, "I am going to move back the hedge in order to have a Church without spot or wrinkle, a mature bride. You must learn to activate your faith and use your weapons of warfare. Warfare is necessary to become overcomers, to be conformed to the image of Christ."

Those who do not understand God's timing and purpose in lowering the hedge will have mental breakdowns and resentment and eventually bitterness will take root in their hearts. They will say, "God, You have forsaken me! Where are Your promises? Where are Your blessings? How could You allow this to happen to me after all I've done for Your Kingdom?" But in the arms of true covenant, Christians can say with Job, "Though He [the Lord] slay me, yet will I trust Him" (Job 13:15).

Allow me to be specific as to the reasons that the hedge is moved back from people in covenant:

1. *To answer the challenge of the devil.* David declared the will of God against Goliath amid the jeers of both Saul's and the Philistine armies. David stood confidently in the authority of God's anointing upon him. Likewise, you must learn the authority of God's Word and use the weapons of your warfare effectively to bring down the strongholds of Satan.

2. *To allow us to develop spiritual maturity.* Esther finally had to confront the king, knowing that she could die with her people. Maturity cannot come as long as God's fence of protection surrounds us. Esther was forced to follow God's will at the risk of her own best interests. Few Christians have come to the realization of "loving not their lives unto death" for the sake of the gospel, but God will call for such confrontations among those whom He has sovereignly placed in key roles in leadership for such a

time as this.

3. *To learn how to fight with spiritual weapons at a new level.* Nothing must hinder you from fulfilling your mission from God. Once the Apostle Paul entered into covenant with God he said, "I was in peril in the sea. I was in peril in the city. I was beaten, imprisoned, ridiculed, physically attacked and left for dead. But now I know who I am and I know where I am going! I have a course to finish!"

Recently I called for God's overshadowing of one of the Church's most revered lyricists, Dottie Rambo, who was facing serious surgery on her spine. As I prayed, God allowed me to see the warfare over the city of Atlanta. This woman's life has been given to proclaiming the gospel in songs of victory and triumph in the power of Jesus Christ. She faced a major test of her faith. Yet God allowed my vision to transcend her particular need to see both eagles and vultures gathering over this city where God has appointed watchmen in His Church. Jesus said, "For wherever the carcass [His body] is, there the eagles will be gathered together" (Matthew 24:28).

WINNING WITH UNCONVENTIONAL WEAPONS

Our warfare cannot be won with carnal weapons. We are spiritual beings with a spiritual mission. Spiritual warfare is won only by the power of the Holy Spirit—and God uses unconventional weapons. Joshua's march around Jericho, David's slingshot used against Goliath, Gideon's broken pitchers of light, all these weapons transcend reasonable strategy in ways to win a military battle. God enjoys winning battles by seemingly ridiculous methods through the obedience of faithful people. Jesus' death on the cross seems to be a foolish way of redeeming mankind from Satan's clutches, but death and resurrection is God's plan of defeat for opposition against Him.

> Then I saw an angel coming down from heaven, having the key to the bottomless pit and a great chain in his hand. He laid hold of the dragon, that serpent of old, who is the Devil and Satan, and bound him for a thousand years. (Revelation 20:1,2)

The believer binds Satan and his forces by the Word of God. You cannot bind an evil spirit with a chain, but Jesus gave you the power to bind and to loose spiritual adversaries that oppose His will. Since *ten* is used consistently in the Bible as a number of completion, ten times ten times ten means absolute completion—or one thousand (years). When you pray in Jesus' name, according to His will, you have the authority to bind Satan completely by the Word of God.

> And he cast him into the bottomless pit, and shut him up, and set a seal on him, so that he should deceive the nations no more till the thousand years were finished. But after these things he must be released for a little while. (Revelation 20:3)

We live in a day in which the nations of the world have an unparalleled opportunity to hear the gospel of Christ. Recent years have proven to be a time of great evangelistic freedom in proclaiming God's Word. People have been given the choice of accepting or rejecting Christ's gospel of hope. I believe that the *release* of Satan for a short time refers to a period when freedom to proclaim God's Word is confined or hidden from an unbelieving world.

Now when the thousand years have expired, Satan will

275

be released from his prison. (Revelation 20:7)

When a thousand years (time of completion) have expired, Satan will be released from the binding of God's Word which has held him on a leash until that time. The Reformation, the Revivals, the Charismatic Movement, all these historical outpourings of the Spirit of God upon His Church have kept Satan bound from totally plundering the earth. But a time will finally come when Satan and his forces will be defined and released to deceive the nations. Please remember that God will allow this release of satanic forces in order for His ultimate purposes to be served. God is always in absolute control, the final authority in heaven and earth.

> . . . and will go out to deceive the nations which are in the four corners of the earth, Gog and Magog, to gather them together to battle, whose number is as the sand of the sea. They went up on the breadth of the earth and surrounded the camp of the saints and the beloved city. And fire came down from God out of heaven and devoured them. (Revelation 20:8,9)

Obviously this passage does not refer to literal Jerusalem because it says that all saints are there. This *city* refers to the place of God's presence, His universal Church. So the people of God are surrounded by these forces of darkness, and fire from heaven devours forces opposing God and His people.

> And the devil, who deceived them, was cast into the lake of fire and brimstone where the beast and the false prophet are. And they will be tormented day and night forever and ever. (Revelation 20:10)

This verse marks the end of human history as we

know it or the end of the age. God's sovereign intervention will designate a finality to recorded history as mankind has experienced it. God now awaits an adequate witness to the gospel of His Kingdom so that He can bring all nations and people into judgment.

SEPARATING THE WHEAT AND THE TARES

Where are we now in this prophecy? Lowering the hedge separates the wheat and the tares (Matthew 13:24-30). Until the generation of the harvest, wheat and tares have grown comfortably together within the Church. For the past two thousand years men and women called of God have sown good seed. Meanwhile, wicked ones have sat comfortably among the company of believers. False teachers and religious hypocrites have sung, prayed and attended church faithfully right beside people who are sold out to the Lord and who seek His Kingdom first. God has allowed this mixture to continue for the sake of protecting His elect from being *uprooted* (Matthew 13:29).

Because the Church is entering the *time of harvest* with the proclamation of God's Word unparalleled since the days of the first apostles, the time of separation by God's *angels* or messengers has come.

The messengers (angels) of God's Word provide the catalysis for this separation in their bold proclamation of truth. When the hedge of protection is lowered, truth serves as a sword which divides. *Tares* react to truth by being offended or trying to persuade people of faith with arguments based on the mind of reason. Jesus explained the parable of the wheat and tares to His disciples by saying that unrighteous people will be cast into the lake of fire, but those who are righteous will shine like the sun. Then Jesus added, "He who has ears to hear, let him hear" (Matthew 13:43).

The story of Israel in bondage in Egypt gives insight into the separation of the wheat and tares. Though the Egyptians used God's people to make bricks and build cities, together their accomplishments were impressive. God allowed this mixture to continue for the sake of Israel's survival and even for the advancement of civilization for several generations.

As the Hebrews worked alongside the Egyptians, we can speculate that some enjoyed good relationships. Remember that Moses grew up in the courts of Pharaoh. He was given the finest education that Egypt had to offer. But the cries of Israel went up before God as rulers came to power in Egypt who did not remember Joseph (Exodus 1:8).

Pharaoh's hostility toward God's people parallels some people's attitudes toward where the Church is moving in prophecy today. Egyptian persecution increased. The bondage of world systems became more pronounced and oppressive upon the people of God. The Hebrews' cries for mercy only increased the cruel oppression of their taskmasters. But God divinely separated the wheat from the tares. The Passover was that sovereign visitation from God that separated those with the blood over their doorposts (Covenant) from those who refused to hear and obey God's voice.

What is the application of the Passover in our modern world? Science and engineering are examples of humanistic kingdoms which have worked beside spiritual healing and God-given creativity to bring mankind to impressive standards in modern medicine and technology. Agnostic psychologists, lawyers, professors, legislators, philosophers, journalists and other professionals have worked beside people who understand and apply the principles of the Kingdom of God. Working together, we have created an imperfect mixture, but also a workable social order. Now finally we have come to the time when God leans over the balcony of heaven and says, "It's time for harvest. The day of mixture must end."

SURFACING THE ISSUES OF CONTENTION

Where will the conflicts be most notable? Where will the separation between wheat and tares be the most pronounced? As God lowers the hedge, how will the issues surface which will separate the wheat from the tares?

1. *The secular media.* Increasingly the Church faces ridicule from the press. Spiritual language always sounds fanatical on the evening news. News feeds on controversy. Because news supposedly emphasizes factual information, any comments spoken in faith or out of conviction sound totally unsynchronized with the journalistic tone of news reporters. The contrast between the reporter's factual statements and commentary and a Christian's answers based on a biblical perspective always presents the Church in an unfavorable light.

Most Christians portrayed on television and in the movies today are characterized by ignorance, legalism and irresponsibility. Sadly, Christians justify the stereotype when we air our differences before the world. We flaunt the failures of our brothers and sisters and demand that they be punished. We promote an *escapist mentality* instead of solutions to world problems. We seem either too naive or too uninformed to give answers to the perplexing issues of our day.

Will Christians be discerning about what they hear on the evening news? Can we effectively use the secular media and the commitment of Christian journalists as a means to witness, to give solutions to the hopeless despair of our world?

2. *Strategy of the mind or strategy of the spirit?* In many ways this distinction in thinking is similar to the problems Christians encounter with the secular media. God's direction is not based on intellectualism, emotionalism or reason. Many Christians will be tested by having to choose between following human logic or spiritual direction. Socio-economic issues will likely force Christians to choose whether they follow the opinions of the status quo or the Spirit of the Lord. As society faces the twenty-first century, will the Church be able to hear God's voice and move in one accord?

3. *The printed page.* Who has the right to print a perspective which he claims comes from God? We have virtually experienced a *book war* in Christian circles the past few years. This war of theological perspectives, biblical interpretation and biblical application will continue.

Permanence and efficient distribution of materials make the printed page one of the most powerful vehicles for taking the message around the world. This fact alone makes the printed page a battleground. Look for a continued battle over the minds of men as the publishing war continues, especially with well-informed readers who are both secular and Christian leaders. Pray that the process of bringing definitions of Kingdom principles into practical application will work to unite the body of Christ. Pray that doors for the gospel will continue to open.

4. *Warfare between old guard and new guard.* Most Christian leaders will admit that when God moves, the greatest opposition to a new move is the previous move. Not only is God moving today, He seeks leadership who will move with Him. Too many times leaders are locked into the glory of previous days. They defend their teachings, their books, their insights which God gave to them twenty years ago. Meanwhile, God's truth marches on. God gives fresh insights and strategic direction which does not con- tradict nor invalidate any previous direction—but only enhances it. Nevertheless, new things threaten the old guard. Anything *new* or unfamiliar is rejected.

5. Another area of contention focusing on God's timing is *passing the baton* to the next generation. Only God can designate the proper timing. Planting or reaping too soon or too late will spoil the harvest. Often young Christians are seizing the reins of lead- ership prematurely. Older men give up too easily in order to retreat to safety and comfort, only to be dev- astated when they realize they failed to complete the task God gave them to do. They realize too late that their mission from God has been aborted—passed on too quickly to those unseasoned in ministry.

Discernment is necessary in knowing God's will concerning when and how to *pass the baton* of lead- ership. Eldership needs to judge in these matters because timing is critical. The true measure of suc- cess is the quality of your successors. Any leader uninvolved in the process of preparing those who fol- low after him is not a true leader.

The last verse of the Old Testament resounds with the prophet Malachi's promise of the hearts of fathers and their children being reunited (Malachi

4:6). The power of that mutual commitment in the work of the Kingdom causes intense warfare over the seed. Wheat and tares will be divided by their commitment to nurturing the seed in the days ahead. Wheat are committed to the future; tares live for their own welfare with little regard for the continuity of history.

6. *Church structure.* Structure implies authority and government. The transcending government of the one Church, the body of Christ on earth, is based on spiritual authority, not organizational structure. Men and women of authority are confirmed by the anointing of God upon their ministries. Such authority transcends denominations.

I foresee a notable decline in denominational structure as the primary power base governing the local church. Increasingly, men and women will know one another by the Spirit, not by the positional structure as we have known in the past. The contention over structural authority will distinguish wheat and tares in the Church. Expect attention focused on this subject in the immediate future.

7. *The ministry of apostles and prophets.* In many ways this issue relates to discussions of establishing structure since the ministry of apostles and prophets has been virtually unrecognized in the modern Church. These ministries are once again surfacing with dramatic benefits. Just as apostles and prophets laid the foundations of the first-century Church which evangelized the world, modern apostles and prophets will prepare and lead a spiritual army in waging war against satanic forces in the final battles before the coming of Christ.

Expect heated discussions over the roles and functions of these callings. Apostles are elders who rule in spiritual matters and establish works for the Lord. Prophets give direction and warnings from God. These ministries are essential to fulfilling the commission of the Church. Some will receive these ministries; others will turn them away and refuse to hear them.

8. *Interaction With ministering spirits.* Intercession is a key element in overcoming satanic powers in spiritual battles. As the warfare increases over covenant Christians who are tested as Job was tested, expect signs, wonders and miracles of preservation. Supernatural beings, angels, will minister to those in covenant with God in the midst of trials (Hebrews 1:14). Some will reject the miraculous interventions of God and explain away any supernatural signs. Others will have their eyes open to realms of faith and God's desire to defend His people, calling upon Him for wisdom and direction. Intervention from God will separate the wheat from the tares.

For you, the separation of the wheat and tares means that you must become like Job in your unbending trust toward God as historical events affecting our civilization quickly unfold. Satan has asked for the same freedom to attack the Church as he had when he attacked Job. This day of our greatest blessings and greatest warfare now presses us to understand covenant. Covenant understanding will enable us to reap the great harvest of the earth amid tremendous calamity.

Our warfare in the United States is accelerating as our government continues to pass laws restricting the voice of the Church. The spirits of atheism, lawlessness and mammon try to dominate our judicial system. Atheistic forces use a strategy of defending individuals' offenses to freedom of prayer or religious expression to prevent causes of God which benefit all of our society. Such warfare will eventually test the martyr spirit in the body of Christ. Who will compromise the truth? Who will stand in such a day of testing?

We will see obvious distinctions between the sons of darkness and the sons of light. Persecution of true believers by religious judges is promised in this day according to God's Word (Luke 21:12). Have we ever known a time when judgments among Christian ministers have been greater? Some religious leaders sit in Moses' seat to judge others. Preachers rail against other Church leaders, pointing fingers, calling names. Religious persecution, even imprisonment and death for a witness to Christ, increases as restraints against Satan are removed. After giving such warnings, Jesus adds,

> Therefore settle it in your hearts not to meditate beforehand on what you will answer; for I will give you a mouth and wisdom which all your adversaries will not be able to contradict or resist. You will be betrayed even by parents and brothers, relatives and friends; and they send some of you to your death. And you will be hated by all for My name's sake. But not a hair of your head shall be lost. In your patience possess your souls. (Luke 21:14-19)

Patience is a key quality in the days of harvest, particularly since Jesus asks the question, "When the Son of Man comes, will He really find faith on earth?" (Luke 18:8). Yes! An empowered Church will await the coming of the Bridegroom.

Loosing of Satan is necessary. I know the battles I face simply by making that proclamation. I've settled within my spirit to stand whatever consequences come. Men who admit that they hear from God face ridicule. When a Christian says that he hears from God, spirits of this world become belligerent and attack him in any way they can.

A cry unto God resounds as Christians must either come into the fullness of Christ, or be destroyed. The Bible says, "For the great day of His wrath has come, and who is able to stand?" (Revelation 6:17). That is the question that every Christian must answer. Many fall away during adversity because they have not been established in the truth of God's Word.

Tribulation separates the wheat from the tares at the time of harvest. Tribulation feels like intense pressure. God is calling for us to be pressurized into making some choices, some decisions. Obviously *pagans*—murderers, thieves and all unsaved people— are already separated. We have no difficulty recognizing those who are openly aligned with world systems. They define themselves by admitting that they do not have faith in God. Separation of wheat and tares occurs in God's house.

> Of how much worse punishment, do you suppose, will he be thought worthy who has trampled the Son of God underfoot, counted the blood of the covenant by which he was sanctified a common thing, and insulted the Spirit of grace? (Hebrews 10:29)

The most tragic separation at the loosing of Satan will be among people who have heard the gospel; some even have understood and have entered into covenant with God, but then they began trampling the blood of Christ under their feet with their presumptuous ways, calling for grace to cover their repeated wrong choices. Covenant with God grants both blessings and curses. For so long God has simply backed off and allowed such prodigals opportunities for repentance. But at an appointed time, God will no longer allow them to trample the blood of Christ, to ignore their vows to God, to abuse their relationships in the body of Christ. God's Word clearly indicates that a day is coming when God's vengeance will be visited upon those who knew truth but turned away in disobedience to His voice.

These are people who knew the principles of covenant with God. Their actions mocked the spirit of grace. They always reasoned, "God understands!" "God knows my problems!" "God will allow me to . . ." And God replies, "You've insulted the Holy Spirit. You have become so fleshly in your goals that you will be called to task in the *Day of the Lord.*"

ATTACKS FROM INSIDERS

Tares are *insiders* in the Church. The Apostle John writes about people committing a sin which leads to death. We are commanded not to pray for restoration in behalf of such a sinner (1 John 5:16,17). Sin resulting in breaking covenant with God, mocking grace and trampling the blood of Christ underfoot is not worthy of our prayers. That sin is the same as blasphemy. When one has so discounted the blood covenant, God will not allow another violation under His longsuffering mercy.

Paul writes to the Corinthians about an immoral relationship in their congregation. The man involved was corrected and given an opportunity to repent, but he refused to listen. Paul instructed the church leaders to turn the man out of the church for the devil to have him (1 Corinthians 5:5). Many times the way to bring correction to someone is to back away and allow the devil to work them over. They quickly become miserable in the sin which once brought them pleasure.

Later Paul wrote to the church leaders that they had left the man alone long enough. He was concerned that the attack of the devil would destroy the man for eternity. He instructed the leaders to bring the man back into fellowship (2 Corinthians 2:1-11). Some people are restored to fellowship in the Church because they long for reconciliation with God and His people. But a time is coming in which many will not be able to know reconciliation. Of these, God's Word instructs, "Don't even pray for them."

> For it is impossible for those who were once enlightened, and have tasted the heavenly gift, and have become partakers of the Holy Spirit, and have tasted of the good word of God and the powers of the age to come, if they fall away, to renew them again to repentance, since they crucify again for themselves the Son of God, and put Him to an open shame. (Hebrews 6:4-6)

I emphasize that we live in a day when these verses in Hebrews will take on greater meaning in the life of the Church. Why now? Because God must bring the harvest time to fulfillment. God requires maturity and righteousness of His Church in order for it to be a witness to world systems. This standard is produced when God looses Satan to come after our homes, our children, our minds, our health and our finances.

Many attacks will come from *insiders* within the Church family. After much reproof, these *insiders* will harden their necks and say, "I understand more than these self-proclaimed prophets. Does only (Moses) our preacher hear from God?" Then come warnings, pleadings, discussions and strong words from the Lord to abate their direction. But they ignore all the warnings and use their energies to wreck God's cause. They never realize that the path they choose will harden and embitter them.

Destructive forces of insiders begin with the mind of reason opposing spiritual direction from God. Satan used the mind of reason to rob Eve, King Saul, and likewise, many Christians today of their original callings from the Lord. A person cannot grieve the Holy Spirit without having enjoyed fellowship with the Holy Spirit. For one to back away from the leading of the Holy Spirit means that he once flowed in spiritual direction from God. A person cannot resist the Holy Spirit unless he has previously been obedient to God's voice.

Some people presumptuously sin by saying, "I know that God's grace is sufficient. He will take care of me. I'll go my way, and God will understand." Quickly their own interests become far more important than God's. Insiders instigate the great battle for God's people in the time of harvest! Those battling from the outside are easily defeated by the power of God because the issues they raise are so clearly defined according to God's Word. Insiders present a much more subtle case. They sound so spiritual and so convincing.

Israel always knew that the Philistines were opposed to God's plan for them. They knew that their unity and dependence upon God would defeat the enemies of Israel. But insiders present a totally different problem. People divide and mumble among themselves. Unity is destroyed as people take sides. Some people who are genuinely seeking truth become confused with numerous voices which all sound right, yet oppose one another. The Bible warns of the destructive power of insiders in the most tragic stories recorded in Scripture.

Cain knew that God required a blood sacrifice, but he decided that he would worship in his own way. He would give God what he considered to be an appropriate gift. Cain's attitude is also reflected in the answer he gave to God's question concerning the whereabouts of the brother he had murdered. Cain's heart had hardened (Genesis 4:9).

Numerous other examples in Scripture of insiders—Ham mocking his father Noah, Rebekah and Jacob's scheme to secure Isaac's blessing, Delilah's betrayal of her lover Samson, Absalom's ambitious plot to overthrow his father David—all demonstrate the tragic consequences of insiders' judgments and taking matters of spiritual authority into their own hands. Insiders always justify their actions as being *the right thing to do.*

The greatest opposition in Jesus' ministry came from Jewish leaders, *insiders* among the chosen people. These were leaders who understood, taught and wrote about covenant with God. They, of all people, knew best the prophecies concerning the Messiah. Likewise, the greatest opposition to the cause of God within His body on earth today will be people who understand, write and teach covenant.

Who was the most tragic *insider?* Judas walked with Jesus, saw Him minister, knew His patterns, even knew when Jesus was most vulnerable to attack. Religious leaders negotiated with this *insider* to work with them in their plot to destroy God's plan. Judas' kiss said to world systems, the harlot Church and the devil, "Here He is! Take Him!"

THE INSIDER'S MENTALITY

Deception overtakes the minds of insiders. Many sincerely believe that they are doing God a favor. They are convinced that they are purifying the people of God by exposing faults. They feel totally justified in their words and actions. And we live in the day when Satan's choice recruits will come from insiders in ministry, leaders in the Church and people who have the confidence of others and the ability to influence them. They do not believe they are wrong.

> And they did not repent of their murders or their sorceries or their sexual immorality or their thefts . . . (Revelation 9:21)

Lack of repentance characterizes insiders in the time of harvest. They see the destruction they cause, but feel totally justified in their actions. Their feelings of compassion are seared so that their only motivation is to prove their point. They are proud people. They hate God's leadership because rebellion rules their hearts. They will relate all the ways they have been *wronged* by leaders in God's house. Their own little groups approve the destruction imposed by one another because they all once knew the foundations of covenant and practiced God's laws. Now they justify one another's grievances.

The army of saints in the great battle at the time of harvest are people who know covenant. The Word of God promises that true covenant people will shine as martyrs and witnesses in this day. The power of Satan will be released upon the Church as it was upon Job. The natural mind will not be able to comprehend the reasons for such warfare. In the heat of battle, God will separate the wheat and the tares which have grown in the same field since Jesus announced, "The Kingdom of heaven is at hand!"

Let me emphasize, wheat and tares grow in the same field. Pressures of life will separate them. The bride of Christ is the wheat. God is finding His bride in the most turbulent days that the Church has ever known. Preparation of the bride requires that she be tested.

The bride of Christ must prove that she will stand in faith amid great persecution. She must prove a trustworthiness in expressing her own desires. She must stand tall in direct confrontations with the enemy. No longer will diverse voices and doctrines toss her to and fro. Pressures from the enemy will produce a righteous people of God, the people who were not a people, and bring us to the marriage vows. The marriage supper with Christ will not occur until the bride has been totally, thoroughly tested.

> Then you say in your heart, "My power and the might of my hand have gained me this wealth." And you shall remember the Lord your God, for it is He who gives you power to get wealth, that He may establish His covenant which He swore to your fathers, as it is this day. (Deuteronomy 8:17,18)

When the law of this dispensation ends, God will take the covering of His grace to a higher level. Tribulation ends the time of grace as we have known it within the Church until now. In the great harvest separating wheat from tares, we find understanding of the parable of the marriage feast (Matthew 22:1-14). Many who are invited to the feast refuse to come into covenant with God. The king was so angry at the abuse of His messengers that He burned up their city (verse 7). We are entering a time of God's sovereign judgment upon those who trample His covenant.

The parable says that those who were invited were not worthy. The messengers were commanded to bid both *good and bad* people to come to the feast. The churches fill as a *wedding hall* fills with guests. That command also gives understanding to the parable of the dragnet (Matthew 13:47-50). That command means that we are in the time of harvest. Suddenly the gates are down. People flood into the house of God where they find a feast, worship and truth spread before them.

Then the king discovered someone who was not in covenant—who did not wear the proper garments. Heed this word! They were in the banquet hall, but they never took covenant seriously. When they wanted to, they observed the Lord's supper and baptism. They tithed if they had some extra money. They honored the leading of spiritual headship if they agreed with what he said. The King responds to such people sitting at His banquet table by asking, "How did you get in?" Then the King commands that these guests be separated, bound hand and foot and cast into outer darkness. Suddenly we understand the significance of the verse, "For many are called, but few are chosen" (Matthew 22:14).

Now God's angels (messengers) are issuing a command to come into covenant with the Lord. Five years ago, this message was only a firstfruit message. Now God's messengers are shouting out His provisions from the housetops. Many men and women of God are bringing understanding to the meaning of covenant today to those who have ears to hear. Covenant relationships, covenant giving, covenant families are the themes of the Church in this hour!

We are coming quickly to the time of marriage. Satan is released and the hedge is lowered by God to finish our preparation to rule worthily with Christ in His eternal Kingdom. Days of intense testing have begun. Be faithful, Church! Satan's final fling will press us to dress in garments for the feast. Beyond the law of grace comes the chastening, the trials and the warfare which will produce a worthy bride.

> Then he said to me, "Write: 'Blessed are those who are called to the marriage supper of the Lamb.' " And he said to me, "These are the true sayings of God." (Revelation 19:9)

The harlot Church is judged at the same time that the bride is purged in covenant. Esther and Ruth are prototypes of the Church. In both stories, the hedge of protection was lowered to test these womens' covenants and faithfulness to obey God in the place of service where He had called them. They both overcame trials and temptations. The covenant Church will not bow or bend under pressure. Insiders will fall as they attempt to use weapons which cannot prosper against the bride. But the Church will stand true to the testimony of Jesus, to the testimony of covenant and to the spirit of prophecy (Revelation 19:10). Church, heed the Word of the Lord!

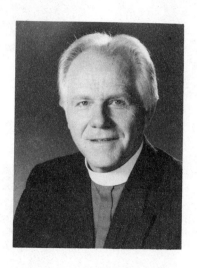

ABOUT THE AUTHOR

Bishop Earl Paulk is senior pastor of Atlanta's Chapel Hill Harvester Church, caring for a parish of 10,000 with a vibrant diversity of specialized ministries. Ordained as Bishop in 1982 by the International Communion of Charismatic Churches, Earl Paulk is called upon worldwide as a spokesman for the gospel of the Kingdom. His television program, *Earl Paulk* is widely viewed throughout the United States, Africa and Latin America. To date he has published ten books, including *The Ultimate Kingdom, Satan Unmasked, Sex Is God's Idea,* and *Held In The Heavens Until.*

Other books by Kingdom Publishers:

To order use form on following page.

Kingdom Publishers Order Form

Please forward the following books to me:

Name _____

Address _____

City _____ State _____ Zip _____

Telephone (_____) _____

QTY	TITLE	PRICE	AMT
	POSTAGE & HANDLING		2.50
	TOTAL		
	BOOK & TAPE CATALOGUE		FREE

Enclose check or money order for full amount
and mail along with this order form to:

KINGDOM PUBLISHERS

POST OFFICE BOX 7300
ATLANTA, GEORGIA
30357

Mail this page for FREE one-year subscription to *Thy Kingdom Come* newspaper.

Please send me:

☐ FREE one-year subscription to *Thy Kingdom Come* newspaper.

☐ A book and tape catalog of messages by Earl Paulk

☐ Please put my name on the mailing list for Earl Paulk Ministries.

Name _____

Address _____

City _____ State _____ Zip _____

Telephone (_____) _____

How did you receive this book?

☐ Bookstore   ☐ Friend   ☐ Direct Mail   ☐ Television Ministry

Mail To:

Earl Paulk
P.O. Box 7300
Atlanta, Georgia 30357